~~Un~~Conditional Love

~~Un~~Conditional Love

Stacey Berger

Write My Wrongs Co, United States
www.writemywrongs.co

Copyright © 2024 Stacey Berger

All Rights Reserved. No part of this book may be reproduced, stored in a retrieval system, or transmitted by any means, electronic, mechanical, photocopying, recording or otherwise without written permission from the author.

Contents

FOREWORD i
Chapter One: Summer 1974 1
Chapter Two: People don't like me because I'm Jewish? 7
Chapter Three: Christmas at Dorado Beach 9
Chapter Four: Introducing the Berger Family 13
Chapter Five: A Famous Chimpanzee, Bat Mitzvah 19
Chapter Six: Down the Shore 21
Chapter Seven: Abington High 23
Chapter Eight: A Close-Knit Family 27
Chapter Nine: Family Rules 31
Chapter Ten: No Boundaries 37
Chapter Eleven: George Washington University 39
Chapter Twelve: Jacob and Martine 43
Chapter Thirteen: A Terrible Premonition 45
Chapter Fourteen: A Family Tragedy Changes Everything 49
Chapter Fifteen: Departed Too Young 57
Chapter Sixteen: 1989—The Aftermath 65
Chapter Seventeen: Another Cruise Already 73
Chapter Eighteen: Off to Law School 77
Chapter Nineteen: Dating and Doctors 81
Chapter Twenty: Physical Aggression 85
Chapter Twenty-One: Haunts Me Today 89
Chapter Twenty-Two: Ship Them Out Again 93
Chapter Twenty-Three: Stress, Engaged 95
Chapter Twenty-Four: Father's Day 99
Chapter Twenty-Five: Mr. & Mrs. 103
Chapter Twenty-Six: The Honeymoon's Over 107
Chapter Twenty-Seven: Violent Endings 111

Chapter Twenty-Eight: New Beginnings- My Josh 113
Chapter Twenty -Nine: Unhappy Families... 117
Chapter Thirty: End of an Era 123
Chapter Thirty-One: Saying Goodbye.. 139
Chapter Thirty-Two: A New Normal 145
Chapter Thirty-Three: My Bari 149
Chapter Thirty-Four: What's Going On? 151
Chapter Thirty-Five: The Letter 159
Chapter Thirty-Six: He's in His Underwear... 165
Chapter Thirty-Seven: I am Punished 171
Chapter Thirty-Eight: Our Jamaican Adventure 173
Chapter Thirty-Nine: Insanity 179
Chapter Forty: Divorce.. 181
Chapter Forty-One: Alone... 185
Chapter Forty-Two: A Vacation With Mom 189
Chapter Forty-Three: Painful Parties.. 191
Chapter Forty-four: Avi and The Needlemans 195
Chapter Forty-Five: Never Good Enough 199
Chapter Forty-Six: Lessons Learned 201
Chapter Forty-Seven: No Reading of the Will? 203
Chapter Forty-Eight: Did I grow up in a different family? 205
Chapter Forty-Nine: The Letter Again 207
Chapter Fifty: I am Done... 211
Chapter Fifty-One: My Reading with Danielle Schwartz, Medium........ 215
Chapter Fifty-Two: Fly Away 223
Epilogue.. 227

FOREWORD

I'd like to get one thing straight before I dive into the story of my extraordinary life: this is not me bragging about how fortunate I was growing up. My father worked hard for every cent he made and insisted upon the very best for his wife and three daughters—and that was precisely what we got. We enjoyed travel, the finest hotels, the best restaurants and theater seats, and were given practically everything our little hearts desired.

We had what most would consider to be the perfect fairytale life.

In this book, I will relive the sequence of extraordinary events that led to this point in my life when I finally decided to put everything down on paper. Think of it as a kind of therapy, if you will. A much-needed catharsis almost forty years in the making.

In delving through my past and that of my remarkable, unique family, perhaps I'll make some sense out of the toxicity that developed between me and my mother and sisters. Sadly, at the time of writing, I barely see my sisters and only talk to my mom during an obligatory call on some holidays.

And you know something? I welcome the peace.

I'm Stacey Berger. I was born in 1967, back when the Rolling Stones were still very much a new thing, and I grew up to become a preschool teacher and a lawyer. I married at twenty-four and am the mother of two wonderful kids who are my whole life. My parents took care of me as a child, and my husband took care of me right after. I never had to worry about paying a bill. I filed for divorce at forty-two, stopped being a preschool teacher, and started practicing law to support myself. I was so scared to be on my own, but I did it. I worked full time, changed my lifestyle, and eventually moved to Miami from the Philadelphia area. Now I sit in my beautiful apartment in Miami, enjoying a comfortable breeze as I look out at the water, and I recall how I've lived and how I've loved.

All in all, it's been one hell of a ride so far. And as the Grateful Dead would say, "What a long, strange trip it's been."

My family and affluent beginnings went a long way toward molding me into the person I am today, but I firmly believe the events that transpired on July 19, 1989, shaped my destiny. Because, as with most fairytale beginnings, things inevitably go wrong—and often in a most spectacular way.

These are my memories.

Memory can be self-centered, egotistical, and exculpatory. Long term memories can fade and dissipate, containing time lags and blank spots. Some memories are completely forgotten. Some people recreate their own self-centered version of the past and believe it.

There may be instances in this book where my sisters, my mom, others in my family—my aunt and uncle, even my cousins—have different recollections of the same event in which we all participated. And while I have tried to talk about my childhood experiences with my mom and sisters, they simply refuse to discuss anything with me. Furthermore, my parents only told me what I needed to know. My thoughts and feelings fill in the blanks for so many of the things they kept secret from me.

And so, my book is deliberately my personal and subjective experience.

Chapter One:
Summer 1974

It is the smile of a child, the love of a mother, the joy of a father, the togetherness of a family.

—Menachem Begin

The last day of Willow Grove summer camp. I was sad camp was over but also excited to go down the shore for Labor Day weekend with my family. For eight weeks, Monday through Friday, I would wake up early in the morning to go to Willow Grove Day Camp and not return until close to dinner time. Some kids rode the bus, while others were assigned a driver. My driver picked up my sister Lisa and me as well as another family of kids from just around the corner of our house.

I was in Aunt Jill's bunk. Our bunk name: Aunt Jill's Jellybeans. All the adults at camp were always called "aunt" and "uncle." There were fifteen of us in the bunk, all six to seven years old. I'm sure you can imagine the fun we had!

My favorite parts of that summer were making the swim team, visiting the carnival, acting in the camp play, and organizing our bunk sleepover. For one night, we were allowed to bring our sleeping bags to camp and stay after everyone else had gone home. There was a big barbeque for dinner, and then we got to go night swimming in the pool!

When you pulled into Willow Grove Day Camp, a big red fire engine greeted you from the playground; you could see it from the street. During Carnival, there was a "marriage booth" on the fire engine. For me, that was the most exciting part of Carnival—finding out who would climb up onto the fire engine to get "married." The lucky ones left with a little piece of paper acting as their "official" marriage certificate. The "ceremony," as well as all the games and prizes to win, made Carnival one of the highlights of the summer.

I also loved playing Newcomb, which is volleyball for youngsters. My serve was amazing and always helped my team win. We played against other bunks and enjoyed intercamp days when other camps would come to us or we would visit their camp to play Newcomb, kickball, swimming races, and other competitions. Things would be even more exciting when one of your friends visited from a neighboring camp!

That year, I was cast in the camp play, which was kind of a big deal. We practiced all summer. At the tender age of seven years old, I played Fifi LaFontaine, who was dressed in white short shorts, a white tube top, white gloves, and a white feather boa. In character, I sang a very sexy song to the camp! The lyrics began with, "I want to do my best for you…"

I think it would all have been considered inappropriate today. Ha!

In addition to everything going on at the girls' camp, it's important to note there was also a boys' side to the camp, which was a form of entertainment for us all by itself! We simply couldn't wait to go see the boys whenever we got a chance! The tetherball courts were on their side, which provided a good excuse for us to go over and spy on them. On occasion, they would even visit and play with us. We also got to see the boys at lunch every day, which made that mealtime extra special.

We didn't bring our own food in a brown bag. We were served a big lunch every day- hamburgers, chicken fingers, cold cuts. I loved the salad; it was probably all watered down, but I can still remember to this day just how much I liked it.

On Fridays and the last day of camp, our driver took us all to 7-11 for Slurpee's. Since we were so young, the excursion was always *so* exciting! On Fridays and the last day of camp, the store was filled with campers.

Going to camp in the summer seemed to be a Jewish thing. Other kids went to the beach or their club or stayed at home with their moms, but only the Jewish kids went to summer day camp. Even today, there are many school-sponsored summer camps, but those aren't the same thing. There are also summer programs lasting a week or two and focusing on science or sports, but this is also not what I experienced. There were about four popular day camps where I grew up, only open for the eight weeks of summer. They had bunks where you had your own cubby, pools, archery, art and crafts, nature activities, dance, and so much more. A kitchen served lunch every day in a mess hall. It was the best.

Unconditional Love

Jump forward two years, and there I stood, aged nine, waiting in a parking lot with my parents along with many other girls and their families. We waited in anticipation for the buses to take us to camp. I was especially excited because it was my very first time at overnight camp, and I was thrilled to be away from my parents and sisters for eight whole weeks!

Overnight camp is very expensive. Today, it costs around $12,000 a summer for one child to go to overnight camp, and somehow it has been reduced to seven weeks, so you understand how much my parents wanted me to have that experience. Some people think Jewish parents are sending their kids away to get rid of them for the summer, but the reality is it's the most spectacular experience for the kids. The whole summer with no TV, no computer, no phones! When my children went to overnight camp, I had to sign a document stipulating if my child got caught with their phone at camp, all confiscated phones would be sent to the Israeli Army. No air conditioning. It was incredible.

Once there, I could call home twice during the whole summer—scheduled calls only, except in the event of an emergency—and only saw my family once, on Visiting Day, throughout the whole eight weeks. The camp I attended in 1976 was Lake Bryn Mawr in Honesdale, Pennsylvania, way up in the Poconos. It was an all-girls, uniform-wearing camp; even our bathing suits had to be exactly the same and from the army navy store.

As was tradition, your accommodation was a bunk or cabin. There was no air conditioning whatsoever, and the bathrooms left much to be desired. However, for my first year at Lake Bryn Mawr, I was placed in a brand-new building they called the Lodge. It was an upscale, much more comfortable cabin with new hardwood floors and floor-to-ceiling mirrors. The best things were the drawers under our beds where we stored our clothes. In an ordinary bunk, clothes were kept in the back of the cabin in little cubby holes with communal shelves for clothes, shoes, bathing suits, and towels. So, when we woke up to a cold morning, I didn't have to run to the back of the bunk, freezing from the cold, and grab warm clothes as fast as I could. I just had to reach over my bed, open the drawer and grab my sweatshirt.

In the Lodge, thanks to those beautiful floors, you could play the absolute *best* game of jacks! And, of course, I beat almost everyone.

One of my other favorite things was Sunday mornings. We were allowed to sleep in as late as we wanted and then headed up to the food hall for breakfast in our pajamas (*no* uniform!) whenever we got up. As we walked in, we were greeted by a huge smorgasbord of breakfast foods, including my favorites—lox and bagels.

Some other treasured memories include when we were woken up in the middle of the night to enjoy an impromptu ice cream party or when our counselor came back from her night off with pizza or Frei Hofer's chocolate chip cookies to share.

Funny, it seems like *all* my favorite things involve food. Ha!

The one thing I did not care for was when the director of camp woke us up every morning to Reveille and directed us to wear the appropriate shirt, shorts, pants, or sweatshirt for the day. They based the decision upon the weather, and all girls had to wear what was called out in Reveille—absolutely *no* excuses! "Good morning, Lake Bryn Mawr girls. It is a beautiful day, and we will be wearing our green shorts and yellow t-shirts…"

Like the day camps, most of the overnight camps happened to be Jewish. There wasn't really anything quintessentially *Jewish* about them, except that most of the kids there were Jewish, and at Lake Bryn Mawr, we would have Shabbat every Friday night. Shabbat is the day of rest in Judaism, which begins on Friday night when the sun goes down and lasts until Saturday night when the sun goes down. At camp, Shabbat meant all the girls had to wear a white shirt. We observed a small shabbat ceremony with the whole camp in the recreation building and then headed to the mess hall for a special dinner, which consisted of roasted chicken, challah bread, potatoes, and some veggies. At Lake Bryn Mawr, we had professionally trained cooks and bakers, and the meals were amazing—especially for camp food!

A couple years later, I graduated to a co-ed camp. Woohoo! It had the girls' side and the boys' side with the added frisson of it being overnight. The possibilities for nocturnal mischief had increased a hundredfold!

"Color War!" The camp counselor's shrill cry rang out through the balmy mid-afternoon air like the call of some strange creature dwelling in the dense woods surrounding the bunks and impressive mess hall. The counselor, Aunt Abigail, was "Mom" to Leah, one of the girls I'd made friends with—it wasn't unusual for parents to work at the camp to pay for their child to attend (a barter agreement for camp tuition)—and she stood out among her teenage colleagues like the proverbial sore thumb. I'd heard her husband also worked as a doctor on the boys' side. A lot of the campers' dads were doctors and would barter the tuition this way. But I couldn't begin to imagine my mother or father flouncing around the camp in bright T-shirts and ill-fitting shorts. What a vision that would have made!

Every one of my fellow summer campers bristled with excitement—Color War! The incessant chatter ceased, and all eyes turned to the plump counselor, who I thought looked particularly sweaty and uncomfortable in her khaki shorts and bright red camp t-shirt; it was a hot, humid day.

As Aunt Abigail's voice resounded, I observed with mounting anticipation as teams formed and the red shirts moved quickly away from the blue shirts, everyone exchanging suspicious glances. The seriousness of Color War settled upon Camp Echo Lark—newly forged friendships were dissolved in a heartbeat depending upon the color of a shirt, and friends and teammates were torn apart by the impending rivalry. At that time, there was nothing quite as important as the week-long event of Color War. Once announced, the bundle of activities that would decide the ultimate winner was all we could think about—I especially couldn't wait for the talent show, basketball and soccer games, tug-of-war, and Rope Burn, as they were all so exciting! The senior boys got to do Rope Burn every year. Everyone gathered down by the lake, spray-painted their hair (parents sent their kids with both colors of spray paint, not knowing what team they'd be on) and applied face make-up with their team colors. Each team collected wood all day for this tradition. Imagine two tree branches dug into the ground and attached by a rope. Each team built a fire below the rope, and the first team whose rope burned first won! Rope Burn was worth a lot of points for your team.

My parents never scrimped on anything and wanted my sisters and me to go to the very best camp. They knew it would introduce us to countless good friends and serve up a bunch of wonderful memories that would last a lifetime. Not once did I ever think of it as my parents sending me away—it was always one of the very best times of my life.

By day, we'd play team sports such as volleyball—my personal favorite—try our best in soccer and basketball. We also had individual activities like swimming, arts and crafts and archery. We would sit during rest time and listen to the older girls as they swooned over the boys they'd claimed to have seen on the boys' side. Although it was a co-ed camp, the counselors kept the sexes separate with all the zeal of prison wardens, for all of the obvious reasons. Our girls occupied the front, and the boys lived farther into the woods. But inevitably and in the time-honored tradition of teenagers the world over, boys and girls would sneak out of their respective areas under cover of night for clandestine romantic clinches down by the lake—we called these excursions *raids*. I was one of those daring campers who made my way toward the lake by flashlight for the excitement of stolen kisses.

It was that same lake where we would enjoy movie nights. It was always some wholesome, family movie a couple of years old, like *Herbie Rides Again*, *Huckleberry Finn*, *Escape to Witch Mountain*, or some other Disney movie. I guess they didn't want to scare the little kids too much. For me, it didn't matter so much what movie was. I cared more about hanging out with my new friends, giggling together, acting like fools to entertain one another, and behaving just as little kids do.

We also had pizza and ice cream nights in the cabins, dressed in pajamas and told stories until we could barely keep our eyes open. There seemed to be no barriers, no judging—everyone saw everyone else on equal footing. We were all just girls together, best friends from the first day. Of course, sometimes we got on each other's nerves or even argued. Looking back, living with ten other girls for eight weeks really taught me how get along with others, how to compromise, how to share bunk chores, and how to be on the same team.

All in all, I had many great times, forged lifelong friendships, and made fantastic memories. And while camp was very much the pinnacle of the year for many other girls my age, for the Berger sisters, it was just the tip of the affluent iceberg.

This, then, was my summer camp: eight full weeks spanning my entire summer vacation in Pennsylvania's Poconos area, which I absolutely *loved* and looked forward to every year until I hit the summer after tenth grade. That's when I graduated to the delights of the Teen Tours and traveling the country with forty teen girls and boys on a luxurious extravaganza! We flew from all different states to meet at the airport in Colorado. We then traveled by bus along the west coast and to many cities in Canada. Sometimes we would set up tents at a campground and other times we would stay in a nice hotel. There were twenty girls and twenty boys on my Baron's Teen Tour, and it was an incredible experience. Years later, my sister would meet someone from my Teen Tour and end up marrying him.

The summer after my Teen Tour, I went to a summer program at Cornell University where I attended class and received college credit while I was still in high school. Again, mostly Jewish kids, and another great experience.

At Cornell, I got caught drinking Tab and vodka (gross!) with my friends. But my mom always said if you get in trouble and tell the truth, you will be in less trouble. So, I called my mom right away to tell her what had happened and that the staff were going to call her. My mom would be great about these things if I told the truth. While I sat at the end of a long table with the teachers who had caught us, the program director called my mom on the speaker phone. To my delight, she listened to them and said, "Okay." That was it.

I also called my mom every time we cut Hebrew School. While many kids stopped going to Hebrew school after their bar or bat mitzvah, I went to the Hebrew High School to be confirmed, as did many of my friends. Sometimes we would cut Hebrew School altogether—when we were dropped off, we would sneak around the side of the building and run to the closest street, Old York Road, then make our way down to the ice cream shop on Elkins Park Square to hang out and eat. It was fun, but before I could enjoy myself, I went right to the pay phone and called my mom to tell her we were cutting school, and I was at Hilary's Ice Cream Shop with my friends. That way, when Hebrew School called to see where I was, my mom wouldn't be mad at me, and I wouldn't get in trouble.

Chapter Two:
People don't like me because I'm Jewish?

I didn't know I was Jewish until I encountered anti-Semitism at the age of 10, when my best friend told me I couldn't come to their house because I was a Jew.

—Peter Eisenman

When I was in second grade at Rydal Elementary School, I sat at my desk as my teacher handed out a math worksheet for each student to work on. I got my sheet, and it was so easy, I completed it quickly, with all the correct answers. Since I had nothing to do, I looked to my left and started talking to the girl sitting next to me. She hadn't finished her problems yet and ignored me. So, I looked to my right and started talking to the boy on that side. The teacher approached and told me to be quiet. Since I had finished my work, the teacher gave me a dot-to-dot to complete. When my mom found out they were giving me dot-to-dots and not something more challenging, she decided to take me out of public school and put me in private school so I could excel at my own pace.

I went to Solomon Schecter, a Jewish day school which fostered my love for learning about Judaism, but it was also the place where I had my first experience with antisemitism. I have very vague memories of a school meeting for the parents at night during which someone bent and broke the antennas on many of the cars and defaced the school prayer books with swastikas. I am not sure I really understood what it meant, but I know I was scared.

Unconditional Love

I also learned about how lucky we were to be able to practice Judaism, whereas Jewish people in other countries, such as Russia, were not allowed. They had to hide in their basements to light the Shabbat candles and the menorah during Hanukah. We studied all the Jewish holidays, so many of which are about someone, somewhere, wanting to kill the Jews, and by some miracle, we always survived.

At the young age of nine, I had firsthand knowledge of antisemitism and clearly understood that some people didn't like me just because I was Jewish. Below is my "Book About Me," which many people also made as children, dated 1976. When asked to imagine a new law, my answer was, "I wish there was a law that said there would be no more hatred of the Jewish People."

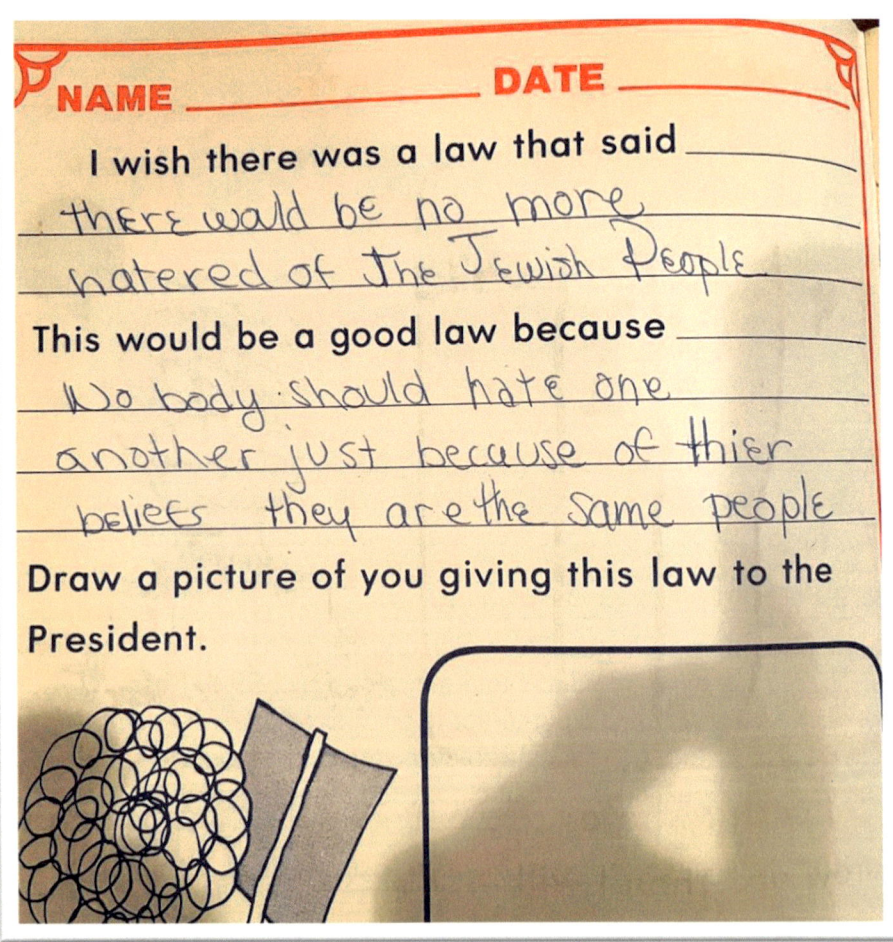

Chapter Three:
Christmas at Dorado Beach

I've had a fairy tale life. I had a perfect family, a beautiful childhood, an incredible upbringing. I lived a lot of life but a lot of good life.

—John Stamos

I was eight, maybe nine, when my parents first took us all to Puerto Rico for the entire two-week Christmas break. While I was accustomed to traveling with my family and experiencing the very best of everything, I was too young to appreciate such a grand, wonderful place as the Hyatt Hotel of Dorado Beach.

Opulent barely began to describe the place. It was a stunning, white stone building surrounded by expansive, sweeping lawns manicured to within an inch of their lives. It boasted sparkling blue pools, beautiful cotton-draped cabanas on its private beaches, countless fancy bars, and restaurants serving delicious foods from around the world—many of the dishes were totally new to me and had names I could hardly pronounce.

The exclusivity of the hotel made it a magnet for the rich, powerful, and famous. At $3500 a night today for the cheapest room, it was certainly out of reach to all but the wealthy. For example, Bob Kraft, the owner of the Patriots, visited Dorado with his family every year during the Christmas holiday. One-year, Happy Rockefeller stayed in the villa next to ours. Being a little kid who was not easily fazed by such things, I took it all in stride and made good friends with the children of those families while the grownups frequented the bars and casinos.

At night, we were 3 girls, after dinner, heading out to the hotel lobby to walk around and look for other kids our age and sneaking into the bars and casino. My youngest sister, Tammy, was too young to do any of these things and being the older sister, I thought that someone needed to watch over her and be a good example. While Lisa was out drinking and hanging out with the other kids our age. (Lisa and I were only 11 ½ months apart), I would stay with Tammy every night. Every night. It wasn't like Lisa, and I took turns, I never even thought to ask. I stayed with Tammy, and I was happy to do so.

It was in Dorado Beach's fancy restaurants where I got my first glimpse of my father's famous temper, which seemed to surface when he didn't get *exactly* what he wanted. The restaurant, as I remember, was where everyone stayed at the hotel and had dinner. As you entered the restaurant, there were five levels, each with tables on both the left and right side of the center staircase. As you walked down, straight in front of you was the ocean, with lights projected on the crashing waves. It was truly spectacular. That restaurant was a favorite of our family, and my father always ensured we got the very best table, on the bottom level, with the best ocean views.

That night, we'd arrived at the main restaurant and, much to my father's chagrin, our table was not ready and had been given to another family. As a small child at the time, I didn't see what the big deal was. Every table had an exquisite view of the ocean. I simply couldn't understand why my father had such a stern look on his face and why he had grown so uncharacteristically quiet.

Later in life, when I learned more about my father, I realized he'd paid off the maître d' to get us the table he wanted at the precise time he wanted—just as he'd paid one of the staff handsomely to take our chairs and towels down to the beach for us every morning—and so he felt he was perfectly justified in losing his temper when he lost "his" table.

Losing his temper in public didn't mean throwing a fit, shouting, or threatening people. No, he was never one to cause a scene. He much preferred to take his displeasure behind the curtain, so to speak. So, upon locating the errant maître d' who had given away our table, my father quietly took him by the arm and led him over to a secluded corner. There, I discovered later, he delivered his rote line in the calmest, firmest manner possible: "Don't take my money if you're not going to do what I asked."

Personally, I'm convinced all recipients of that condemning sentence from my father would have preferred a public scene. At least that way, there would be witnesses to my father's behavior. The cold, quiet tone of his voice was far more menacing than any amount of shouting or carrying on could ever be.

Needless to say, we got our prestigious table that night—and every other night my father requested it during our fabulous stay at Dorado Beach that year and the many years to follow.

Whenever we went to any other hotel, my dad had to investigate all the rooms, so my parents left my sisters and me in the lobby with our luggage while they traipsed around the entire hotel to choose the one my dad wanted. Then they would summon us to bring our bags and head to our rooms.

The craziest story is when my parents went to Las Brisa's, another exquisite hotel, in Acapulco. My dad insisted on sleeping with a breeze, but after looking at all the rooms at the hotel, he couldn't find one with doors or windows in the bedroom to see and hear the ocean. The living area was the only part with doors that opened to the balcony. This is the absurd part: the hotel switched the bedroom and the living area to accommodate him. They had to unscrew the headboard to move the bed. But my dad was happy, and that was all that mattered. (I wonder how much money he slipped someone to have the room remodeled!)

Sadly, as my sisters and I grew older and entered teenagedom, Puerto Rico became less safe for young ladies of our age, so the Berger family embarked on high-end cruises for our family vacations. Naturally, my father approached the cruises with his usual shtick —introducing himself to the dining room captain and our assigned waiter. He even insisted upon seeing the following day's menus each evening so we could order what we wanted in advance. And if there was nothing we liked on a particular day, my father would approach the captain and tell him what we preferred instead. In addition to the daily menu, my dad ordered Caesar salad and fettuccini alfredo many nights for an appetizer. The requested amendments to the ship's menu were always put into place, thanks to my father's usual practice of "taking care of people."

My dad was a perfect example of the phrase "Money talks."

Over the years, before I was married, I have traveled with my family to St. Thomas, St. Maarten, St. Lucia, St. Kitts, St. Croix, Anguilla, Barbados, Antigua, Martinique, Jamaica, Curacao, Mexico, Panama and the Panama Canal, Nevis, the Cayman Islands, Puerto Rico, Costa Rica, Cartagena, and Hawaii. I was very lucky.

Chapter Four:
Introducing the Berger Family

> *I really can't complain about anything. I'm living a childhood dream, and I have a perfect family. There's really nothing that I'm disappointed with.*
>
> —Tim Hudson

Before I go on with more tales of my family and the fortunate life, I enjoyed pre-1989, I think introductions are in order.

We are a Jewish family living in the suburbs of Philadelphia. My mother is Janey. My sisters are Lisa and Tammy. I am the eldest of the three, Lisa is eleven and a half months younger, and Tammy—the baby of the family—is four and a half years my junior. My mom was and still is a stunning woman and extremely intelligent. My sisters are also pretty like mom. Lisa was more of a tomboy growing up, and Tammy was the creative artist.

And, of course, there was my father, Barry. An average height, solidly built, traditionally handsome man, he was the archetypal patriarch of the Berger family. He was a self-made man who'd earned his money the hard way in landscaping; he'd begun on the very bottom rung of the ladder back in his youth, cutting lawns and providing basic maintenance to pay his way through college, Penn State. My parents were especially proud of the business they built together, Barry's Green Thumb. The business would eventually stop providing maintenance services and focus solely on landscape design. When new developments were built, my dad would work with the sod guy, the stone guy and anyone working at the site.

Unconditional Love

We all played our part in my father's success—he'd have had it no other way. While he loved to provide his family with the very best of everything, he also believed everyone had to pull their weight. My mother ran the entire business, taking on all of the behind-the-scenes functions such as payroll, taxes, accounts, and acting as my father's secretary—all of which she did with both aplomb and ruthless efficiency. As for us smaller Bergers, our chore was to work on our father's designs, and we spent many an hour erasing his pencil marks and drawing leaves and fancy stones onto his blueprints while he worked hard during the day and caught up with sales calls at night.

Barry's Green Thumb grew and so did the client list. Occasionally, my dad would landscape for someone famous. One time, Teddy Pendergrass's people called and asked if he would work his renowned magic on the singer's grounds. It was an opportunity not to be missed, an absolute honor, right up until the point at which they asked my father, "How much will *you pay us* to work on Mr. Pendergrass's home?"

My father never did reveal the reply he'd given Pendergrass's people, but it was no doubt incredibly blunt yet professionally courteous—something like "I get paid for my work." Although the offer was an outright insult, Barry Berger was not one for burning bridges when it came to business. Though he never did work on Pendergrass's landscaping.

He also landscaped for Lisa Thomas Laury, a Philadelphia news anchor, and one of the Caputo brothers, whose father was a famous Philadelphia criminal defense attorney.

A funny story involved Irv Eatman, who played for Philadelphia's semi-professional football team, although my dad had no idea who the man was when his "people" called to ask if he would create something spectacular around Irv's mansion. When they met, my father had expected Mr. Eatman to be a small, old, Jewish guy instead of a black mountain of a man getting out of his car.

My father worked so hard to give us a good life that he barely saw us, except in the winter when he didn't work at all. Because he spent almost every day in dirty work clothes and drove a battered old station wagon, my father loved to shop at Boyd's—*the* most exclusive store in Philly—for tailor-made suits and expensive silk ties from Italy. He was proud of his suits and wore them with style. Oh, how I loved to shop there, too. I received extra-special treatment when I mentioned I was Barry Berger's daughter.

My relationship with my sisters involved me, the eldest, taking care of them and making sure we listened to our parents. My sisters used to play outside while I stayed in and helped my mom make dinner or read a book. One time, Tammy asked Lisa, "Why do you listen to Stacey? I know I do because she's so much older than me. But why do *you* listen to her?" Lisa didn't have an answer. They always played separately from me, since we were very little. It was almost as if *they* were eleven and a half months apart, not me and Lisa! At my bat mitzvah, Lisa only came up to my shoulders—I was so much more mature and looked years older than her. In their speech during my wedding, my sisters said, "We were always lucky to have Stacey as a sister because any time our parents asked for one of us to come help, Stacey would jump up and say, 'Here I come!'" That sums up our dynamic.

When my dad took my sisters and me shopping, he loved the excitement of the deal and saving money, even if it was only a few bucks. He attempted to negotiate with the poor teen shop assistants at the mall's chain store outlets—the Gap used to be one of my favorites—and I'd stand beside him, mortified, as he tried to make a deal. Of course, the assistants were in no position to do anything of the sort and, try as they might, they were unable to convey that to my father in a way he'd understand.

And so, in a huff, rather than pay for the clothes I'd picked out, my father would go to one of his favorite exclusive stores and pay ten times more for the same thing. That way, even though he still wanted to negotiate a little off the price, the shop owner was ever accommodating and my father left delighted.

My parents even taught me how to negotiate. As we went into a jewelry store with my dad, he said to watch and listen. That at one point, if they do not lower the price we are asking for, we were going to say no and walk away. They stood strong on their price and dad secretly nudged me to follow him to the door. Right when we were almost at the door, he said, they would call us back and lower the price. And that was exactly what happened.

Despite spoiling me with everything I wanted, my parents instilled some good, solid financial practices in me. I was always taught to save, save, save. While we drove around, I remember my dad showing us someone who lived in a big house and drove an expensive car. He explained the man could've had no money in the bank *because* of that house and car with the old saying "You can't judge a book by its cover." People are showy, he said, and want you to think they have money, but you never know how much money they really have. He was very much a "rainy day" kind of guy—someone who saved and always looked forward.

His financial philosophy stuck with me throughout my life. He taught me to save and never throw money out. In seventh grade, I bought my very first boom box—a radio you could carry around—with my Bat Mitzvah money. Before I could buy it, Dad made me study the Sunday paper every week for a whole month to compare and find the best price. I reported back to him with the research I'd done, and, after the month, we compared the prices in all four weeks and decided where I should make my big purchase. It annoyed me at the time—I was an impatient teenager who just wanted her music right then and there—but when I got a great deal by biding my time and shopping around, I truly appreciated Dad's guidance. Those are lessons I never forgot and still practice today.

Our family revolved around my dad and his work, and we were all happy to oblige. However, Mom really ran the show at home. Together, my parents created this beautiful family filled with happiness and love. And I felt lucky.

As it was all I'd known, I saw nothing wrong with spending all my social and spare time with my mother, father, and two siblings, or the fact we were all expected to be perfect, shiny, beautiful, and "on show" always. I was proud of my family and didn't mind how close we were.

I always had the most beautiful clothes—designer labels, of course—dolls and toys, and a brand new car for my sixteenth birthday. We wanted for nothing at all. Being the oldest of the Berger girls meant I occupied more of the family's perceived spotlight and so the pressure was on me to be even more shiny and beautiful than my sisters. And while I embraced my parent's expectations, my eating habits were most affected.

It was a double-edged sword: a pampered young girl who absolutely loved eating out at exclusive restaurants with all the gloriously decadent fine foods they had to offer. Our absolute favorite was Italian food. From a young age our parents had us eating foods that most children wouldn't even try. I still recall with a fond smile how my littlest sister would refer to mussels as "strongs." We regularly enjoyed fresh lobsters, "strongs," clams, crab, and scallops.

One time we dined at the Blue Bell Inn, a very popular restaurant for special occasions, and my parents told us we were going to have the best chicken for dinner. Occasionally, sitting at the table, by dad would "ribbit,", like a frog. And a few minutes later he'd "ribbit" again. Little did we know that we were eating frog's legs! And we loved them.

It all went together with living the privileged life my parents worked so hard for and managed with such fine detail. We attended shows, concerts, and theater performances, and we were *always* in the first few rows; I cannot remember a single time in my life when we didn't have a perfect view of the stage! As an extra-special treat, my parents would take us all to Atlantic City, or "down the shore," where we owned our own condo on the beach in Margate. We frequented the swankiest casinos even though my father never, *ever* gambled. He was so vehemently opposed to it that when we lived in Atlantic City, when the casinos were being built, he would drive us around to point out which of the boarded-up businesses had been lost to gambling.

It was a stark lesson that stuck with me, and one he hammered home again when, aged twelve, I won sixty dollars of nickels on the slot machines in Puerto Rico. Far from being pleased with my big win, he took every one of those coins from me and threatened if I *ever* gambled again, he'd send me home to my grandparents!

At the casino restaurants in AC, we were treated like VIPs—all thanks to Barry Berger and his generous palm-greasing. I saw countless amazing shows there: Liberace, Chicago, Diana Ross, Whitney Houston (back before the drugs took hold and she *really* could hit the notes!), and not once did we ever have to wait in line to get in. As we approached the theatre, a long line was wrapped around the corner to the right, everybody waiting to see the big show. We would walk past the entire line and Dad would tell us all to stand over to the left and wait. He would walk through the closed curtains and disappear. After a few minutes, my dad would peek his head thought the curtain and gesture for us to come…we were always guided by the well bribed door staff through the VIP curtain and into a high-roller booth; to say we felt like royalty would be an understatement!

To the eyes of any young girl growing up, her father is usually beyond reproach. Mine was ostensibly a saint of a man: hard-working provider, loving father and husband. My mother was beautiful, intelligent, and a loving mother and wife. They never gambled, drank alcohol (I saw him partake of a glass of whiskey only three times my whole life! And mom drank once a year on New Year's Eve, that was always fun!), smoked cigarettes or pot, and was unerringly faithful to each other.

Throughout my whole life, we only ever had a relationship with Dad's side of the family. My mother didn't talk to her own mother at all, nor to her sister Judy or any other member of her family, except for her sister Heidi, who lived in California. Sadly, I never knew my aunt Judy, but I thought she and my grandmother must not have been nice people if my mom could ignore her own flesh and blood. My mom was an incredibly judgmental person who had an uncanny ability to cut people off and carry on with her own life as if they'd never existed. It was part and parcel of her existing within a small, sheltered Jewish bubble. This was not unique to my family. It was very much a Jewish thing for family members to refuse to speak to each other. Unfortunately, I didn't understand how restricting and damaging such a life can be until I got divorced and dared venture out into other communities, which weren't as judgmental.

When my grandmom, my mom's mom, passed away, I was shocked to see how much my cousins loved her. My aunts and their kids came to our house. My cousins cradled special blankets and stuffed animals my grandmom had given them, crying at her loss. I didn't have a blanket or stuffed animal and didn't feel any such remorse, except for the fact that I hadn't really known her. Clearly, my cousins loved her and had had a special relationship with her. Because my mom had cut her off, my sisters and I hadn't been able to speak to her either. I refused to repeat this behavior with my own children. Today, I don't really speak to my mom or sisters, but I encourage and respect their relationships with my kids. It is not for me to take that away from them.

Chapter Five:
A Famous Chimpanzee, Bat Mitzvah

Everything we did as a family had to be the very best, and money was never an obstacle. Once, my parents had a birthday celebration for Dad that was certainly no exception. They threw a huge party in our backyard with a tent and a live band. It was an adult party, and I was probably about 10-12 years old, but I was allowed to invite one friend—my best friend, Kim.

The coolest thing at this party was that one of the bartenders was the one and only world-renowned star Mr. Jiggs! He was perhaps the most famous chimpanzee of the seventies, known across the country as the model for Polaroid camera advertisements and featured on the popular TV show *That's Incredible!* He wore a tux and smoked cigarettes just like a human, and he played the conga drums better than anyone I'd ever heard! I cannot imagine how much money it must have cost to have the world-famous chimp and his owner, Mr. Ronald, all the way from New Jersey to bartend at Dad's birthday party!

I'm sure many people know a bat mitzvah is a *huge* deal for every twelve-year-old Jewish girl. It marks the beginning of womanhood, and we prepare by studying the Torah, or the five books of Moses, for a year in advance of our big day. When I was that age, girls were not called to read from the Torah on a Saturday morning, when the scroll is ceremoniously brought out of an ark. Girls were only allowed to read from the Haftarah, which is a series of selections from the books of Prophets, after the Torah reading. Those selections were typically linked thematically to the weekly Torah portion. I was proud to be one of the *first* girls allowed to read from the Torah in the synagogue on a Saturday morning.

Nowadays, *all* girls are permitted, but back in the day, I thought it was something special.

My Bat Mitzvah was a black-tie Saturday night affair. Dad landscaped the entire inside of the synagogue—*our* synagogue—with live trees twinkling with thousands of Christmas tree lights. To achieve this, he'd had to transport a whole bunch of trees into the synagogue and put lights on them on Saturday, which was the Shabbat. Working on Shabbat is simply not allowed in the Jewish faith—*nobody* is permitted to do so. It is a day of rest. The rabbi knew Dad had planned to decorate the place, but told him he was not, *under any circumstances*, allowed to do any work on the Shabbat! But since not all rules applied to Barry Berger, he went ahead and did it anyway. And he made that synagogue look like a wonderful, sparkly fairy world for my very special night.

My day was amazing. I read from the Torah perfectly—all my practicing paid off—and the celebration that night was spectacular. It's not uncommon for kids to make bank at their bat or bar mitzvahs, especially those of us with well-connected parents. Sadly, as is the custom, we rarely see any of the money because most of it is taken away by our parents and tucked away for college.

After the evening, we were, without ceremony, thrown out of the synagogue for Dad's indiscretion! Thankfully, Mom quickly found us another synagogue—there were *three* near our house to choose from—and we moved to another which was right down the street. There are three different types of synagogues Jewish people can attend: Reform, Conservative or Orthodox, with Reform being the least strictly observant and Orthodox being the most. I was brought up Conservative, and I still am today.

Chapter Six:
Down the Shore

Enjoy the little things in life, for one day you may look back and realize they were the big things.

—Robert Brault

My family absolutely *loved* going down the shore to Margate, right outside of Atlantic City. When I was young, it was a vibrant place with a predominantly Jewish and Italian population. Going "down the shore" was a colloquial phrase denoting a trip to Atlantic City and its famous beach. My sisters and I grew up going "down the shore."

Crime plagued plenty of areas in Atlantic City even before the arrival of the casinos and all the unsavory characters they attracted. So, we vacationed in Ventnor and Margate, which were more high class and filled with much nicer people—the kind of people my parents were happy for us to mix with. I was never allowed to go to Wildwood, an area where tons of kids walked down the boardwalk and, on the beach, —but my parents would say, not Jewish kids. I was forbidden to go there, and to this day, I have never been.

Mom and Dad loved Margate so much we graduated from the White Sands Motel to our own beachfront condo in Margate. My parents eventually added two more condos to our portfolio within the same building.

Dad loved the breeze. Prior to buying the condo, he researched which direction the wind blew, and which side of the building received the most air. As a result, he purchased the right corner apartment on the top floor, which we named

Breezy Point. As a Father's Day present, we engraved the name on a brass knocker for the front door.

We went out as a family every night when we were down the shore. I don't remember my parents ever getting a babysitter and leaving us at home to go out with their friends. We went to Atlantic City to go out for a fancy dinner and then walked on the boardwalk to get Steele's fudge and play Skee ball in the arcades. We went to the Ocean City boardwalk to get pizza at Mack 'n Manco's, see Mr. Peanut at the peanut store where we would get hot roasted peanuts and go on as many rides as I wanted. Some nights, way after our bedtime, we would go out for hot fudge sundaes at Two Cents Plain where there was always a long line to get in. My sisters and I would lay in bed while mom read poems from *Where the Sidewalk Ends* and passages from our favorite books like *Mr. Bump* and *The Stupid's Step Out*.

We went to the beach all day, swam in the pool and always got a special treat when the ice cream man walked by or when they were not allowed to walk on the beach anymore, rang the bell from the steps to the beach. I always got a chocolate fudgsicle, sometimes I'd get the red, white and blue ice rocket or a choco-taco.

I grew up with so much love and so many happy memories. I was happy and I was loved.

Mom NEVER cooked down the shore! Not even breakfast. For breakfast, there was a little restaurant in our building that would also have a long line to get in. My mom would call from upstairs and let them know we were coming. We would go downstairs, excuse ourselves to the front of the line, and walk directly to our table. We never waited in line and if my dad couldn't pay someone off to take care of us, we wouldn't go to that restaurant. Simple as that.

Chapter Seven:
Abington High

There were three different high schools in my area growing up: Abington, Cheltenham and Lower Moreland. I went to Abington. Our school was comprised of three demographics—the Jews, the black kids, and the white kids. All the Jewish girls and boys from each school district knew each other from Hebrew school and the area's three big synagogues. It was how we all met and formed friendships—some that would last us through junior high, high school, and sometimes for a lifetime.

I invited girls from all 3 schools to my Sweet 16. After the all-important milestone of a Jewish girl's bat mitzvah comes the equally significant sweet sixteen. If anything, it's more a coming-of-age ritual than the reading of the Torah, even though it has nothing whatsoever to do with religion—or even being Jewish. A sweet sixteen is almost exclusively a girl thing. All the gals would get together for a luncheon of tea and sandwiches at someplace nice: not quite Fridays, but more like high tea at the Ritz Carlton, especially for the wealthier young ladies. It provided an opportunity to dress up and indulge in sumptuous food and salacious gossip.

Inevitably though, my parents went way over the top with *my* sweet sixteen—nothing but the very best for their little girl! Instead of high tea at the Ritz, we held my celebration at the Philmont Country Club, which was one of the poshest, most exclusive country clubs in the suburbs of Philadelphia. The event, complete with a live band, lasted an entire Saturday night. The best part for me was each girl I invited was allowed to bring a date! As an example, an invite had been addressed *to: Julie Rubin and Date.* Since when did we ever get to go on a date at sixteen?

The girls from Lower Moreland had absolutely *everything* and were far more precocious when it came to money and material things. Once, I went to a bar mitzvah for a Lower Moreland boy from camp. He was a year older, but I was his girlfriend, so I was invited. I didn't really know anyone, but I was still so excited to be there. I listened to all the girls complain their eyebrows hurt. I could not figure out why your eyebrows would hurt until someone told me they'd had them waxed. They were twelve and thirteen! I didn't know about such things at twelve! As a party favor, we received custom tan shirts printed with "Maz's Mitzvah" in brown writing, something I had never seen before. I cherished that t-shirt.

We didn't have as much contact with the Lower Moreland kids as much as we did with the Cheltenham kids. Abington and Cheltenham attended many of each other's parties and hung out together more often. There was an old saying back in the day: "Date a girl from Cheltenham but marry a girl from Abington." I'm not sure if it also applied to dating and marrying guys, but the man I married, Jon, was from Cheltenham. Maybe it did because he ended up cheating on me before I divorced him. Perhaps I should have heeded that old saying!

It seemed all the Cheltenham kids grew up much quicker than those at the other two schools, but they had so much more fun! They drank, smoked pot, and fooled around with each other much sooner than we Abingdon students did. As a matter of fact, my very first cigarette, the first time I smoked pot, and the first time I messed around with a boy were all with my friends from Cheltenham.

We Abington kids were different from the Cheltenham lot. Our parents were way stricter for a start. As a result, we were prissier. I visited friends' houses in Cheltenham where they smoked cigarettes in their rooms or joints outside. Abington parents would *never* allow that. It was shocking to witness at fifteen or sixteen years old! If I wanted a cigarette or weed, I felt like I had to go to another state with a complete change of clothes and make darned sure my hair didn't smell.

One thing I can say, though, is Cheltenham girls were so much wiser to the world, especially when it came to dealing with boys. I remember clearly one night at the Old York Road ice rink talking to a girlfriend from Cheltenham, who I'd gotten to know well at Hebrew school.

"Where did you disappear to, Sherry?" I asked after she'd vanished without a trace from the rink for a good fifteen minutes, and I'd been getting worried about her.

"I went outside with the boy you saw me talking to," she told me with a smirk.

"You went out to smoke without me?" I said, naïvely. "Does he have pot?" I glanced at the boy in question, a scrawny seventeen-year-old who sat in the corner with his friends.

Sherry shook her head. "No, Stacey, I was giving him a hand job behind the building."

"What's a hand job?" I asked, genuinely in the dark. I was *so* prudish, I'd never actually seen a penis before, let alone *touched* one! And he'd pulled it out in public?

My friend Jenny rolled her eyes at me, laughing, and proceeded to give me a fully detailed rundown on the art of hand jobs and what they entailed. I was absolutely mortified. The whole sordid thing seemed disgusting and pointless to me at the time.

That memory highlights the main difference between the girls from the two schools—and the more I hung out with the Cheltenham kids, the more I learned.

At Abington High School, the black kids and the Jews stuck together. The white kids didn't like either of us. I guess they considered me to be one of the "jappiest" of all the girls. JAP means Jewish American Princess, and I was one of their main targets. They were physically aggressive. When I walked down the hall, someone would come up behind me and slam me into the metal lockers with their shoulder. This was a weekly occurrence. But any time someone was about to beat me up, one of my black girlfriends, whom I'd met through cheerleading, would come to my defense. I don't know what I would have done without them.

The white kids also threw pennies at the Jewish kids at lunch. This behavior was still happening when my son went to Wissahickon High School, many years later, but given inflation, the kids flung quarters instead. My son and his friends collected all the change and put it in their tzedakah boxes. A tzedakah box is a container for collecting charitable donations. The Hebrew word *tzedakah* can be translated to *philanthropy*. Many Jewish homes have tzedakah boxes, as they are given out to the kids at Hebrew school. When my son and his friends had filled their boxes with the bullies' quarters, they gave them to our synagogue to donate to a charity in Israel.

Looking back, the weirdest thing to me was that my parents never did anything about bullying. Even when my mom said she was going to call the school, I was so afraid I begged her not to. A big calendar hung on the refrigerator in our kitchen, and I would write at the bottom, "Stacey will be dead." Despite being hated and physically attacked for my religion, I had to go back to school every day and just take it. This is how most Jewish people handle antisemitism.

In fact, when my son was called a "Jew boy" at ten years old on the basketball court, I still tried to be sympathetic. A group of boys, including my son and one of his best friends, who was Italian, were playing basketball at recess. My son and his best friend had an argument over a certain play and in front of all the other boys, his best friend called him a "Jew Boy." Instead of going to school or confronting his parents, I repeated the same behavior of my parents. This friend did not know what he was saying and was clearly repeating what he heard at home. We can't change what people say or do in their homes. We can only make sure our kids are okay. I assured my son the boy was his friend and that he must have heard it somewhere. I explained, even though some people do not like Jews, he should be proud of his heritage.

Chapter Eight:
A Close-Knit Family

A close family is a knit-sweater of warmth, care, and comfort, a nurturing and forgiving environment. Enmeshment in a family can be a rigid filter of control, a controlling and unforgiving environment.

—Will Curtis

Over the years, I've learned there are families, *close* families, and my family. What I'd grown up believing to be the normal way family members interacted with one another turned out to be very abnormal.

We had money, a father who worked to provide for the family he adored, beautiful clothes, sumptuous food, vacations to exclusive resorts, and everything our little hearts desired. Sure, my dad had his quirks—but doesn't everyone's parents? —and a particular way of demanding the best from his wife and daughters. At the time, I chalked that up to him being a man intensely proud of what he'd achieved, keen to show it all off to the world at large, and only truly happy when he was with us.

For the Bergers, we did everything as a family, which meant we had to do everything around my dad, and I do mean *everything*. As a youngster, I assumed all families were the same and that was just how life was supposed to be. It wasn't until high school, when I saw the freedoms my friends enjoyed, when I questioned the way my parents ran our family—and understood for the first time the way in which discipline was meted out to keep me under control was nothing sort of *weird shit* by anybody's standards, and it was suffocating.

On Sundays during football season, I got to go to all the home games with my dad since we had season tickets. However, we had to watch every *away* Eagles game with Dad too, which meant either going to the home game or watching the away game at my parents' house. As a teenager, I could never go and watch the Eagles with all my friends at someone's house. Even after I got married, my husband had to watch every away game with my dad because my dad took him to every home game.

We were huge Philly sports fans, and going to the games with my dad was always fun. For Sunday home games, I got picked up early from Hebrew School to go watch the Eagles. The first thing we did on our way was grab hoagies to eat at the game. Then we pulled up to the stadium like my dad was someone famous. As soon as we approached the parking lot, he merely had to sound his car horn three times by the fence and the parking lot crew would come over and literally open the fence to produce a front row spot my dad could back into. There were only two spots there and another family from my neighborhood, the Merions, pulled in right next to us. Not only did he pay these attendants off, but he also brought them hoagies every Sunday, and they loved him.

But I mentioned I was never allowed to watch an Eagles game with my friends. It didn't matter to him that we wanted to make our own plans as teens craving social lives, friends, and boyfriends. It simply wasn't an option in Dad's mind—we were to spend every Eagles game with him. It was the same for everything. Everything we did, we did as a family, and we all embraced this love and togetherness, not knowing anything different. Watching the game with my friends and without him was not something I could even imagine broaching with Dad—I just wouldn't know *how*. I was able to talk to my mom, but she reiterated that watching the games together made my dad happy and he did so much for us and…

I talked to my friends at school quite matter-of-factly about how my family operated at home. I had no idea at all I was the odd one out by having such strict, controlling parents. By seventh grade, word had spread about Stacey Berger's father and the boys caught on. When I was twelve years old, the boys made up a story that my dad had secreted a zapper in my bra as a deterrent to over-keen wandering hands. The boys staggered around me in the hallways, clutching their chests and making odd buzzing noises through fits of giggles. One of my girlfriends finally let me in on the secret and the reason behind it, and I was absolutely mortified. Years later, they made up a story about prom night. For prom, a lot of the kids in my school go down the shore after prom. The boys would laugh at me and ask me if my dad would be flying over the beach, in the "Berger

Unconditional Love

Helicopter" to make sure I wasn't getting into trouble. The kids knew how controlling my parents were and let me know!

    I sucked it up and waited for my peers to move onto some other poor sap to poke fun at. I learned the hard way not to divulge any more details of my family life to even my closest friends.

Chapter Nine:
Family Rules

Discipline and punishment went together with my parents' strict regime and, again, I considered their methods to be quite normal at the time. As with any errant teenager, breaking curfew was as big a no-no as it was inevitable. But unlike my friends whose parents always showed remarkable leniency, if I dared to come home five minutes after 10 p.m., I would be grounded for weeks and have my phone privileges revoked. In effect, I would be kept in isolation for weeks over a minor infraction of only a few minutes. But as my parents declared, we were supposed to be home five minutes *before*, not after. After all, "If you're not early, you're late!"

And then there was the "no phone calls after ten" rule: friends were not permitted to call the house after 10 p.m., and if they did, I would be punished. I remember asking my mom how I was expected to have any sort of control over when my friends decided they wanted to talk to me. My parents would tell me to "get the word out," and that was that.

Sometimes, punishment would be a good old-fashioned spanking over the knee, which was often preferable to the prolonged torture of missing out on social time, confined to my room. But the problem wasn't so much the discipline Mommy and Dad dished out; it was the excessive control they exerted over us. Teenagers need privacy and space to figure themselves out and develop their unique personalities—a concept that seemed lost on my parents.

My mother, for example, would go through my school bags, read any notes from friends I'd accumulated at school, and listen in on the (before ten o'clock!)

phone calls I had with friends, which were more than stifling, even for someone used to it. And if we were caught doing anything deemed to be "wrong," my mom or dad would be quick to dish out what they considered an appropriate punishment.

One time, for example, I didn't put my freshly laundered clothes away *just so*—and I mean not a sock or pair of panties out of place—and my dad dumped my clothes from their drawers onto the bedroom floor. All of them!

When I was very little, my dad punched a hole in my bedroom door during his legendary rage, during which he shouted at me for something I'd done months before, as if deliberately stoking his anger. When he was furious, I hid in my room.

Then there was the time, when I was in fifth grade, when I failed a test on *Language for Daily Use*. I'd achieved a remarkably unspectacular 55% and attempted to hide the paper in my bag, which was foolish I knew, given Mom's penchant for searching my schoolbag most evenings. I remember how mad she got, her beautiful, perfectly made-up face an alarming shade of red as she screamed at me. I was in my room and went out to her calling my name from the bottom of the stairs. She had the test in her hand.

From the top of the stairs, I tried my best to protest, to tell her I'd studied really *hard* for the test and hadn't been distracted by friends—it was nothing more than an anomaly, maybe even a marking error on my teacher's part. But she saw straight through my lies and, in her temper, threw my *Language for Daily Use* hardback schoolbook up the steps, right at me!

Out of the three of us, Lisa got in the most trouble and talked back to my parents, which only served to further enrage them. I would get so upset and cry in my room whenever Lisa got in trouble, but Lisa never cried. Ha! My parents said they had to come into my room after punishing Lisa to comfort me and let me know she was okay.

This smothering strictness left me with issues that followed me into my teenage years and taught me how to be sneaky. Not long after I started smoking, I learned how to cut into the insulation in my closet and hide my contraband cigarettes in the wall.

As older teens, we had to go into our parents' bedroom upon returning from a night out—no matter what the time—wake Mom and breathe in her face. Literally! That way, she could tell if we were smashed, drunk, or had been smoking cigarettes, and then she could deliver punishments as she saw fit. Lisa very quickly learned Doritos could mask any tell-tale smells and she'd get away with it. She never got caught, unlike me, who thought a stick or two of spearmint gum would do the trick. As my friends would say, I was always punished.

I lived through it all, and, to me, it was just our way of life. I thought we were a happy family, and I was excited to be able to spend so much time with them. I didn't know how unhealthy it really was. I was proud of my family and how close we were. We were special, and I was very lucky.

Mom reiterated that our dad was a good man even though he was prone to outbursts and despite his odd quirks. She told us the good outweighed the bad and Dad was a truly good person.

But one time, when Dad discovered a moldy cucumber festering at the back of the refrigerator, he went crazy. He dragged a kitchen chair in front of the open refrigerator and sat there throwing old food around the kitchen—Mom was in big trouble. Multiple times, upon finding anything sitting on top of his work message book by the kitchen phone, he would throw everything on the counter to the floor. Nothing was to be placed on top of his message book.

Looking back from a grown-up, parent's perspective, I guess it's safe to assume my father needed everything to be in order the way he wanted it. When us girls started driving, he drew up a map of the driveway and labeled where we were each supposed to park!

When I was maybe eleven, we had a family movie day which began with a meal at a diner in the northeast. After a delicious cheeseburger, I ordered the strawberry cheesecake—it was a special and the menu description sounded so mouth-watering. Sadly, the cheesecake didn't quite live up to the menu's hype, and I didn't care for it because it had this awful, thick layer of sour cream on top. But when I told my parents I couldn't eat it, I received the short reply, "You order it, you eat it!" No waste.

The combination of the dreadfully gloppy, gross sour cream and tasteless cheesecake and my parents' lack of empathy made me dig in my heels even more. I refused to eat the damn thing, no matter how much mom and Dad tried to cajole me. At the end of the meal, when it came time to head out to see the movie, the cheesecake remained untouched, save for that first—and only—mouthful I'd taken.

As punishment, it wasn't just that I wasn't allowed to go to the movies with my family. Oh no, that would not be enough. Instead, they took me to my grandparents' row home in Northeast Philly, which was nearby, where I was ordered to go straight to my grandparents' bed, lay down, and stare at the ceiling for three hours until the movie finished, and everyone returned from the theater. Uncle Sammy, my dad's brother, was there and he made me look at the ceiling for a while but then let me off the hook for the rest of the punishment so long as I got back into place by the time my parents returned.

Another time, my sister ordered devilled clams and crab at Abe's Seafood House—another one of my family's favorite places to eat out, a restaurant patronized almost exclusively by Jewish and black families. My parents questioned her ordering both, and she vehemently insisted she was starved and would eat it *all*. My dad reminded her that she can order whatever she wants, but she must eat it. My sister's eyes were too big for her belly, and she was not able to finish her plate, but that was unacceptable. My dad made her eat the rest until she threw up! His philosophy was he'd worked damned hard for the money we were spending, and to waste food would be akin to throwing cold, hard cash into the trash along with the leftovers. He didn't care what we ordered, but we had to eat it. No waste.

Mom had a most unusual relationship with food. She enforced dad's "eat *everything* on your plate" rule—even liver (which made me physically sick!) and the vegetables I hated. If I didn't eat my veggies—asparagus and beets were especially unpopular—I had to sit at the kitchen table until bedtime staring at my plate as it grew colder and less appetizing. Can you even begin to imagine *cold* canned asparagus? Sometimes, my mother or father would put *extra* on the plate, like some form of cruel torment, and I'd have to either eat it or sit with it until it was time for bed.

And because of Mom's obsession with food and our weight, there was never any bread on the table during dinner and there was most certainly *no* dessert! Mom worked diligently to ensure both she and her daughters presented the very best, flawless appearance always. She rarely ate to maintain her slim, gorgeous, movie-star figure and looks. However, she did indulge in buttered popcorn, hot wings, and vanilla icing, and it was fun to watch her eat when she did. Normally, we had half a grapefruit, melon, or a salad as an appetizer before every dinner. Although, I don't think my mom ever took that off her dinner plate and ate dinner afterward. She always said she ate while she was cooking. She chewed her salad appetizer while the rest of us tucked into a sumptuous dinner, but she never actually partook of the main course itself. She did love to eat but told us you had to sacrifice to be beautiful.

I vividly remember one evening, when I was in sixth grade, crying on my bed because I thought I was a little too chubby. Mom sat on the side of my bed and told me that if she thought I was happy being a little chubby, she would let me be. But she knew just how unhappy I was because I had gained some weight…

As I got older, her restrictions became so normal that I simply accepted it as the way things were, not realizing Mom and Dad were instilling me with some serious eating disorders. Right up until I was in my thirties, I couldn't bring myself to order what I *really* wanted for breakfast. Since my mom only ordered egg whites with veggies, *no* potatoes or toast, and only sliced tomatoes, I felt like I had to order the same thing, and I was always starving when I left the table. Ha!

But when I reached my mid-thirties, I finally started to order what I *really* wanted: a cheese omelet and potatoes, well-done. Maybe even some rye toast if I was feeling especially decadent. My mom and sisters would still eat only fat-free everything: fat-free cream cheese, fat-free sour cream, you get the picture. When we chowed down delicious latkes, or fried potatoes, they only ate them with fat-free sour cream.

Are you kidding me?

We are eating fried potatoes—I wanted *real* sour cream!

At the table, Mom and my sisters tried to convince me how good the fat-free sour cream was. Not for me, it's not!

Bagels and lox with fat-free cream cheese? *Please!*

They would not buy regular sour cream or cream cheese for me. One time, I even brought real cream cheese in my pocketbook to my sister's house because I knew we were going to have fish and bagels, and I did not want fat free cream cheese.

As I grew and became more aware of how other families functioned—as in, with completely different dynamics to mine—I often wondered why my parents were so strict, always obsessed with how we looked, how we behaved, our manners, and controlling our every move. My mom even made me walk up and down the hallways with a book on my head for good posture. As to how much of it came from Dad, and how much came from Mom, it was impossible to tell.

Despite all the control, coercion, and manipulation, I grew up with a strong sense of family and never felt unhappy or forced into spending time with them.

We were what I now know to be an "enmeshed family."

Chapter Ten:
No Boundaries

In an enmeshed family, there are no boundaries between family members. Instead of the strong bonds that signal a well-functioning family unit, family members are fused together by unhealthy emotions.

—Rhonda Lewis

As with all great men, my dad did have a secret vice, although he didn't keep it *too* secret; he even went so far as to involve me. He loved women, although he never once strayed outside his rock-solid marriage. Instead, he enjoyed viewing the female form by watching pornography. How would I know this?

At the tender age of seventeen, I worked at a West Coast Video store. I got this job because one of my dad's customers owned it. Yes, my parents made all three of us work to earn our privilege and learn the value of a dollar—I even missed out on the Live Aid concert in Philadelphia because I was on the work schedule and my parents wouldn't allow me to take the day off.

My father would regularly, discreetly, ask me to bring home the X-rated adult movies for him. This is a lack of boundaries. And as the happily obedient daughter, I did exactly as he asked without even questioning it.

He even had a favorite porn star back then (should I really know that?)—the effortlessly nubile and questionably aged Traci Lords. I believe he saw every one of her movies during my time working at West Coast Video, every single one signed out with great embarrassment by yours truly. At that time, you had to go into the back room of the video store to get those movies, and I would ask my manager to go in and find Dad one he liked. Really inappropriate.

Another time when I was much older—I think I was married—my parents took us to a nude beach in St. Maarten. Looking back, I think that's extra weird! But I did learn that nude beaches aren't about seeing sexy naked bodies, but old hairy sunburned naked people, which is kind of gross if you ask me.

This is a perfect example of an enmeshed family with no boundaries. I never even realized how bad it was until I became an adult and told someone how my dad used to make me bring him home pornos. I was laughing as I related the story, and the other person was not. Their reaction was a surprise to me, and I became a little embarrassed.

When we were younger and spending Christmas at Dorado, one night of the vacation, my dad would tell us not to come home before 11pm. That's weird right? So, we would sit in the lobby until 11pm and then venture back to our room.

Chapter Eleven:
George Washington University

College is the best time of your life. When else are your parents going to spend thousands of dollars for you to go to a strange town and get drunk every night.

—David Wood

I studied at George Washington University for my four-year bachelor's degree in business administration. It was expensive, but my parents made sure I had no student loans hanging around my neck and plenty of money to live well. However, I had to keep a journal to record every penny I spent. I diligently noted every dinner with Julie and movie with Jennifer for my dad to review later. After the first couple months, we came up with a budget.

My father claimed there were strings attached to my education fund. But there was one string, and it was a huge one. I had to always maintain top grades. As were expected, Bs acceptable, and Cs meant I'd be returning home. I *always* got good grades.

I studied ardently. I left the library at night with my backpack and headed over to the Exchange, the bar where my boyfriend DJed. I stored my books behind his booth and pushed through all the people waiting for a drink. When I ordered, the bartender served me right away. Sometimes I held an empty pitcher of beer high in the air behind everybody waiting, and the bartender reached over the crowd to fill it up. My friends and I were close with the bartenders, bouncers, and DJs at the Exchange.

Unconditional Love

As a freshman, I did not get into the "cool" dorm and was placed in an upper-class dorm. We had a kitchen, private bathrooms, and showers. This was where I met my roommate Jennifer, from Boston. Junior/Senior year at GW, a lot of students moved out to Crystal City because it was a lot cheaper than living in DC. Jennifer and I were the few that were lucky enough to have our own apartment in DC, right at the bottom of Georgetown and next to GW's campus—paid for by our parents—living the high. During college, I never had to pay for anything – not rent, not clothes, not food- my parents paid for all of it. And no school loans.

I spent close to $70 for a haircut in Georgetown in 1986. However, I felt like one of the poorest kids at college. I got to know students who had *way* more money than me, and I compared myself to them and didn't truly appreciate what I had until much later in my life.

Jennifer and I moved into an all-furnished apartment, but everything was old and ugly. Jennifer wanted to have the sofa reupholstered. I said, "Great idea," and called my mom, who suggested instead I use a sheet and safety pins to fix it up. I wasn't going to be able to contribute and would have to disappoint Jennifer. I was so upset. Who knew how lucky I really was to be living in an apartment in Foggy Bottom?

For Spring Break, I didn't go to Fort Lauderdale or other Florida beaches like most college kids. I went with Jennifer to the Bahamas one year and to Mexico another. I also went on a cruise one year with Julie, a best friend from college and high school. (and Hebrew school, overnight camp and eventually law school) I stayed at the very best hotels for the week with unlimited funds. My parents paid for all my vacations and provided me with spending money.

I still loved to eat at the very best restaurants. It was Julie's birthday, and I wanted to take her somewhere special for lunch. We went and dined at the Four Seasons. Seriously? Who did we think we were? Ha! We smoked a big fat joint before we went, and we were so high. The waiter came over with white gloves, tongs, and a sterling silver tray piled with various breads and rolls and asked if we would prefer onion, pumpernickel, or sesame.

Julie answered, "Yes, please."

The waiter replied, "Which would you prefer, ma'am?" and Julie again answered, "Yes, please." They went back and forth three or four times, and we looked at him like he was crazy until we finally figured out, he was giving us a choice.

Julie and I also liked to go to this French café late at night after the bars had closed and get eggs benedict. Or we would end up at Little Tavern, which was like White Castle, to eat greasy hamburgers while homeless people slept outside.

In some ways, though, my parents' over-protective nature was a blessing to me, despite the fact it made me entirely dependent upon them long after I left home. And I don't just mean dependent on money, but dependent upon their love and acceptance. Wanting to please them so much and to never disappoint them.

My parents were as controlling about my finances as they were about my social life. For example, when I was in college, I got a part-time job because I wanted some more spending money, but Dad categorically refused to allow me to work when I went off to college. He insisted I focus entirely upon my studies, and he made sure I had more than enough money to comfortably live off throughout college.

But don't think I was a goody-goody who obeyed my parents' every whim. I explored my wilder side plenty of times—only never under their ever watchful, controlling eyes.

When I was nineteen with a year of college under my belt, I stayed in the Margate condo with Jennifer, my college roommate, who flew in from Boston for our big weekend in Atlantic City. Mom and Dad were absent because it was Visiting Day at my sister's overnight camp. So, it was just the two of us, and we were so excited for this golden opportunity! Jennifer and I prettied ourselves up—we may have gone a little too far and looked more like streetwalkers than a pair of college gals—and hit the casinos big time.

As the night progressed and we downed cocktail after cocktail, Jennifer and I found ourselves in the ostentatious Trump casino. Since we weren't there to gamble, merely to look incredibly cool, we drank our way through the bar until eventually winding up in the lounge.

That's where we met the band.

I have no idea what the band's name was. Jennifer and I were *so* impressed to be getting hit on by a real, live band, and it didn't matter if they weren't on their way to becoming the next Van Halen. The members chatted us up like we were supermodels and bought us copious amounts of shots. It wasn't long before a lengthy line of upside-down, empty shot glasses ran down the bar. Each one meant another drink was coming, and Jennifer and I were well on our way to wasted.

At three in the morning, the band invited us to an after-hours party at the casino. How could we possibly have said no? So off we went, two naïve college girls not knowing what to expect. It turned out to be a high-roller party with more lobster and shrimp than I'd ever seen in my life, along with endlessly flowing champagne and so many beautiful people—it felt like I'd died and gone to hedonistic heaven!

As the party was in full swing and Jennifer and I were swept up in the novelty, I thought I heard my name over the hotel's intercom. At first, I figured I'd imagined it or perhaps misheard the announcement over the hubbub and loud chatter.

Then I heard it again.

"Will Stacey Berger please go to the hotel phone?"

My heart jumped to my throat and my stomach sank. I knew it could mean only one thing…

Dad.

We did not have cell phones then and my parents had returned early from my sister's camp to find Jennifer and me missing from the condo in the small hours of the morning.

To say he was fuming would be an understatement. I quickly went to find the hotel phone, I was scared, embarrassed and in shock. When I picked up the phone, I heard the unmistakable anger in his voice as he explained to me how he'd called every casino in Atlantic City to find me. He ordered me to stand on the street corner with Jennifer and wait for him to pick us up—*now*. He hung up without saying goodbye, and I knew he'd be on his way soon.

That was how my college roommate and I wound up standing on the side of the road in Atlantic City in the early hours of the morning looking like a pair of drunken hookers.

My dad didn't care one bit that I had a friend with me. He wasn't one to pull his punches just to save me from embarrassment. I told him, "Everybody my age is up now" I had already spent a year away at college and nobody told me when I had to come home. Seething, he drove us around and pointed out all the bars that had already closed. He couldn't find anybody else out partying. He demanded to know why the hell we'd been at the casino until four o'clock in the morning.

I was mortified, to say the least. Poor Jennifer must have apologized a thousand times.

Next week, the same band took a bus from Atlantic City to Philadelphia to meet Julie and me. Jennifer had already flown back to Boston. Julie and I were both back in Philly for summer break. Julie and I drove out of the suburbs to an area of Philadelphia we'd never seen before to pick the bandmates up at the bus station and spend the day with them. It was the first time either of us had been to a bus station.

Chapter Twelve:
Jacob and Martine

My parents met Jacob and Martine on a cruise before I was born. After a couple days at sea, Dad found himself in the elevator with a huge mountain of a man who stood an easy six-four. Dad, at five-eleven and wearing his Jewish star around his neck, felt more than a little intimidated, especially when the giant asked him in a thick French accent, "You Jew?"

The way Dad told the story, he honestly thought he was about to die as the man towered over him, his face stern. But Dad being Dad, he stuck out his chest and replied proudly, "Yeah… I'm a Jew."

At that, Jacob pointed to himself and declared, "Me Jew, too."

From that moment on, Jacob and my dad were firm friends, as were Mom and Jacob's lovely wife Martine. As a foursome, they *clicked*—it was as if they'd been destined to meet all along.

Jacob and Martine were incredibly wealthy and lived in Paris, which I thought was *so* cool. One year, they gifted me an expensive red LED digital watch, the likes of which had not made it to the USA by then!

The two became very special to our family. They also had three daughters, who were a little younger than my sisters and me—we still got along famously, though—and as we became close friends, we grew to love them like family. Jacob and Martine played an impactful role in my childhood, and I have so many fond, happy memories of time spent in their company. We would travel with them, from when we were little, and meet them on a cruise or in Puerto Rico. They also came to stay at our house many times, before and after having children.

Chapter Thirteen:
A Terrible Premonition

Premonitions are there to prepare you for what's to come.
—Stephanie Arnold

So weird that this is Chapter 13. The number 13 is synonymous with bad luck. It's considered unlucky to have 13 guests at a dinner party, many buildings don't have a 13th floor, and most people avoid getting married or buying a house on a day marked by this dreaded number.
—Remy Melina, "Why is 13 unlucky?"

In 1986 on the day of Yom Kippur, my uncle Rabbi Kenneth Berger—Dad's middle brother—wrote a beautiful sermon in the wake of the Challenger disaster that shook the world. He called it "Five Minutes to Live," and based it upon the terrible rumors that the seven poor astronauts who died on were still alive when the shuttle exploded and had time to contemplate their fate as they plummeted toward the sea.

I couldn't even begin to imagine.

In fact, Uncle Kenny's words were so poignant a great many people have asked for a copy, and it was made available for anyone who wished to seek solace and gain an insight into his optimistic attitude toward life.

Our family had little idea just how poignant Rabbi Berger's sermon was to become…

Unconditional Love

It begins:

Dear Friends:

The scene still haunts me: It was perhaps the most awful moment of the past year. Against the pale blue sky on a crystal-clear Florida day, the space shuttle Challenger *exploded before our very eyes. Seven brave astronauts who just a few hours before were chatting with the press, schmoozing with proud relatives and friends, were suddenly gone.*

I bring this to your attention because life and death is a major theme of Yom Kippur. We read in our Mahzor:

Who shall live, and who shall die?

Who shall attain the measure on man's days and who shall not?

On Rosh Hashanah, it is inscribed and on Yom Kippur, it is sealed.

This is, indeed, a time for "Heshbon Hanefesh," for self-introspection. The old adage "Here today—gone tomorrow" is indeed true. Just ask husbands, whose wives are suddenly taken: Wives, who suddenly find themselves alone, reaching over to find the other side of the bed cold and empty...

Now, it was discussed, that death had only come when the capsule hit the water. For perhaps as much as five minutes, the astronauts were alive and conscious and yet knew that death was certain.

The thought terrorizes me. Can you imagine knowing that in a few moments, death was imminent? What would we think of, if God forbid, you and I were in such circumstances? What would go through our mind? What went through their minds, the seven astronauts?

Unconditional Love

Excerpts from my Uncle Kenny's sermon, "Five Minutes to Live", Yom Kippur Day, 1986:

Chapter Fourteen:
A Family Tragedy Changes Everything

We are all just a car crash,
a diagnosis,
an unexpected phone call,
a newfound love,
or a broken heart away from becoming a completely different person.

How beautifully fragile are we
that so many things
can take but a moment
to alter
who we are
for forever?

—Samuel Decker Thompson

It was July 19, 1989, a date I'll never forget as long as I live. It was the day my wonderful, happy life changed forever.

I was twenty-one. I'd graduated from George Washington University earlier that summer and was looking forward to heading off to law school in Boston at the start of next term. I'd moved back home to Philly after college and was delighted to be living once more with my loving family, enjoying the precious times we shared together.

Determined to make the very most of my break, I quickly fell into the routine of hitting the bars virtually every single night with my old high school friends. We'd picked up where we'd left off before going our separate ways to college.

Thursday evening meant a trip to the Irish Pub in the city, and I was busy getting ready for another night of drinking and partying. I sat on my bedroom floor blow-drying my hair in front of my closet's mirrored doors, when I heard a knock.

Before I could say, "Come in," Mom opened the door and walked in, which she always did. I saw straight away something was terribly wrong. I'd never seen her face so gloomy and ashen before.

"What's going on, Mom?" I asked.

"There's been a crash," she told me. "A plane…"

My mind whirled—Dad was safely downstairs, and I knew my sisters weren't flying anywhere—so I had no idea who she meant.

"Uncle Kenny and Aunt Aviva were flying back from vacation on the airplane… your cousins too."

My heart sank as my thoughts sped to poor Uncle Kenny's family, but I was sure they were fine.

My mother shrugged. "We don't know yet," she said quietly. "I just got the call from Pop-pop. The plane went down in a cornfield somewhere near Sioux City in Iowa. We must go to Mom-mom and Pop-pop's house."

I shook my head—I had plans and didn't realize the enormity of what Mom was telling me. "I'm going out tonight," I argued. "I'm going downtown with Julie and Bernadette." I still thought everything was going to be fine.

"No, Stacey," Mom said firmly. "We're all going to Mom-mom and Pop-pop's—*now*!"

Normally, I'd have protested more, but the look on her face told me it would be futile. Because of my youthfully optimistic outlook on life and the fact no one had said anyone had died in the plane crash, I honestly thought everything would be all right after all, and I would miss going out with my friends for nothing. Although I was angry, it was clear she wasn't going to let me leave.

My grandparents lived in northeast Philadelphia, in what we call a "rowhome," which was kind of like a townhouse but not quite so affluent and not as opulent as my family home. But it was a lovely place, nonetheless, nicely furnished and sweetly decorated. My parents had bought this for my grandparents because they wanted to take good care of my grandparents—my parents supported them through the family business, so they never had to worry about money.

We arrived at Mom-mom and Pop-pop's house to find them both in a terrible state. At that moment, I realized Mom's insistence had been the right thing. My grandparents needed their family around them, not only for love and moral support, but to help with the grim but necessary task of calling around the hospitals in Sioux City for any news of crash victims and potential survivors.

Mom called United Airlines—it was their flight that had gone down—and, once she got past the automated messages, was told there was no information yet and relatives of the passengers would be notified in due course.

"You *must* know something," Mom pressed, and I could see she was trying to keep as calm as possible. She clearly understood there was nothing she could do but keep calling back every hour. It wasn't like Dad could grease any palms to get beyond the airline's stock replies.

"No news yet," Mom told my grandparents when she finally put the phone down. "I'm sorry."

"They say no news is good news," I told my family with an encouraging smile. Everyone was beside themselves with worry, and I was doing my best to stay positive. "I'm sure they're all okay."

Uncle Sammy and his new wife Tris, lived in New York, but they drove to Philadelphia that night. The entire family had gathered around my grandparents, waiting for any information we could get.

The next morning, after a sleepless night interspersed with calling the hospitals and United Airlines for news, Tris and I drove Dad and Uncle Sammy to the airport. (not sure why my mom didn't go instead of me?) They were leaving for Iowa to find out for themselves what was happening and if their brother and his family had survived the crash.

Back in those days, you were allowed to walk all the way to the gate to see family and friends board the plane. Tris and I accompanied my dad and Uncle Sammy to their gate, only to be confronted by a sea of reporters. News of the accident had spread like wildfire, and they were all clamoring to interview any relatives of passengers on that ill-fated flight. Even though Uncle Sammy knew absolutely nothing about what had happened or the fate of his brother's family, he answered their questions all the same.

We watched the plane leave with heavy hearts and a little dread. The very thought of losing someone in my family in such a terrible way hung over me. I worried about my dad and my uncle flying and was relieved when I heard they'd landed safe and sound in Iowa.

Little did I know, it would be three months before my dad returned home to Philly.

We didn't find out until five days later that Uncle Kenny and Aunt Aviva had been killed outright when the airplane hit the cornfield. I later learned they were crushed to death. Two of my three cousins had been on the flight. Fifteen-year-old Avigial—Avi—had been thrown out of the plane when the force of the crash had broken her seatbelt and landed in the cornfield. Jonathan, just eight years old, had also been propelled from the aircraft, but when the rescue teams found him in the cornfield, he remained in his seat with his seatbelt intact. Poor Jonathan had broken almost every bone in his body, but the seat had cushioned and protected him. Ilana, thirteen, had not been on the flight because she was away at Camp Ramah, a Jewish overnight camp in the Poconos mountains.

Randy, a close friend of my uncle's family from Tampa, immediately flew up to my parents' house in Philadelphia from Florida. From there, he proceeded to Camp Ramah to pick up Ilana. She needed comfort from a family friend, someone she knew well.

Avi was in a coma for three long months, and my dad stayed with her in Iowa the entire time she was unconscious. He bought a cassette player and played Milli Vanilli tapes—her favorite singers—on a constant loop. The doctors had advised him there was a good chance Avi could hear what was going on around her, and talking to her and playing her favorite music might help her wake up.

One time, early in Dad's vigil by her bedside, she opened her eyes. He told me later that day when he called home how excited he'd become. He called the doctor and nurses in to see, only to be informed it was nothing more than a reflex and a common occurrence in coma patients. They also urged him to not get his hopes up too high. Undeterred, my dad saw it as an improvement in her condition and a sign his dear niece would be on her way to making a full recovery. He never was one to give up on family.

During his three months at the hospital, Dad's inimitable charm compelled all the nurses tending to Avi at the hospital to take care of him. Some brought his laundry home with them and returned it clean and crisply ironed. Others cooked him homemade dinners and baked goods. Typical Dad—he made friends everywhere he went. Years later, one of the nurses from the Sioux City Hospital flew all the way from Iowa to Philadelphia to attend his fortieth birthday party!

From further afield—Nebraska, in fact—a Hassidic Jew named Mendel rushed to Sioux City to volunteer at the hospital, and that is where he met Dad and Uncle Sammy. Mendel stayed with them through that difficult, terrible time and became great buddies with them. It was a friendship they never forgot.

Mendel also came to visit my family in Philadelphia for other simchas—Jewish parties and celebrations. The definition for the Hebrew word *simcha* is *gladness* or *joy*. When Jewish people attend weddings, bar mitzvahs, and birthday parties they call it a simcha. Mendel sent me a gift for another simcha, the birth of my son. It was a beautiful tzedakah box, which my son still keeps, at twenty-eight years old, in his apartment on the windowsill.

As time passed, more details emerged about United Airlines flight 232 from Denver. We found out an engine had exploded mid-flight, and for forty minutes, the passengers were told to prepare for a crash landing. Afterward, during which time there was very little the captain and crew could do to prevent the inevitable, the airplane hit the cornfield and exploded on impact—112 people in all were killed that night, including my beloved uncle and aunt. My cousins had been extraordinarily lucky to have survived.

Forty minutes…

My mind spun back to the poignant piece Uncle Kenny had written about those five minutes the ill-fated *Challenger* crew had to contemplate their own demise and make peace with the death they knew awaited them once the shuttle's cabin hit the ocean. When I'd learned that, five minutes had seemed like a heck of a long time to grapple with such a thing, so I couldn't even begin to imagine what forty minutes must have felt like for all those poor people on board the plane.

When Randy retrieved Ilana from camp and brought her back to Philadelphia, all she knew was there had been a plane crash and her brother and sister were badly injured but alive and being taken care of in hospital. Just like the rest of our family, she had no idea whether her mom and dad were alive or dead until almost a week afterward. I honestly don't know what could have been worse for Ilana: the thought of her parents being dead or the false hope they might somehow have survived the accident like Avi and Jonathan.

My cousins were left without parents.

With Avi and Jonathan in the hospital, Ilana had no place to go—her family had been devastated overnight. Naturally, we assumed she'd stay with us. But Randy had a different idea.

"Ilana belongs back in Tampa. All the kids do," he told my family. Clearly, he believed we would see the common sense in the idea. "They need to be in their home community, where they'll be surrounded by people they know and who love them as their own."

My parents had always been viewed as the caretakers of the family—they'd looked after everyone in one way or another over the years—and felt it was their duty to step in for my cousins in their hour of need.

Randy still insisted upon returning my cousins to their Tampa community. He even suggested that my grandparents move there with them to support them. But none of his plans were even considered. From day one, my cousins were going to live with my parents and become part of my family, and that was *the end*. Knowing my parents for the kind-hearted, nurturing souls they were, I understood why Uncle Kenny would want his children to live with Mom and Dad in the event of a tragedy befalling him and his wife. I don't know if that was outlined in my aunt and uncle's will, I just assumed it because none of this information was ever shared with me. Everything was always a secret, and I never asked. As I grew up, my parents and I had a silent agreement—they would tell me what they wanted me to know. If they didn't share, I couldn't ask about it. Uncle Kenny knew my parents would provide for his children, love them, and give them the very best in life.

But as you will see, that is not what happened at all.

I assumed my aunt and uncle's will stipulate my parents as the caretakers of their children. It saddened me to think of anyone writing a will and bequeathing their own children's upbringings to someone else—it's something many of us do, of course, but always with the understanding that it's "just in case." Because catastrophic events never *really* happen to regular people like us, right?

The whole terrible episode had a profound effect upon me. Sure, I was a grownup, but I wasn't immune to vivid, terrifying nightmares for a long time after that night. Knowing the airplane had erupted into a ball of flames the second it hit the ground convinced me Uncle Kenny and Aunt Aviva had burned to death—the most horrific way I could ever imagine dying. In my dreams, I sit right there on the plane with them when it hit the cornfield, and I'd hear the horrifying screams as searing flames shot through the cabin and people caught fire.

I'd wake up drenched with sweat, my own scream caught in my throat, and I swear to this day, I could *smell* the burned flesh clinging to my nostrils.

A month after the crash, with Dad still in Iowa with Avi and Jonathan, and Ilana living at our family home, we received my aunt and uncle's belongings, which had been retrieved from what remained of the crash. Among the sad collection was Aunt Aviva's pocketbook, which showed no sign of having been burned at all. The authorities informed us that Kenny and Aviva had been crushed immediately upon impact and had thus been spared the fireball. The knowledge helped alleviate my recurring nightmare a little, and I could only hope my aunt and uncle's deaths had been quick and merciful.

The crash inquest revealed the aircraft had not only suffered the engine blowout, but the landing gear's hydraulic system had failed at a critical moment when the pilot had attempted an emergency landing. The plane had somersaulted across the field like a giant, hideous firework, breaking up as it did so. The passengers seated in the middle of the plane walked away with little more than cuts and bruises, and the pilot somehow survived too. Those at the front and rear of the plane—like my aunt and uncle—were not so lucky. Whoever not burned alive or crushed were flung out into the cornfield; only a few of those managed to survive, including my cousins.

The pilot became a hero—the crash could have been a whole lot worse had he not kept a cool head and performed a near textbook emergency landing. It was thanks to him anyone at all survived flight 232 from Denver.

Unconditional Love

Aviva and Rabbi Kenneth Berger, rear, died in the recent United Airlines crash in Iowa. Injured were Jonathan Berger, front left and Avigail, front right. Daughter Ilana was at camp in New England when the crash occurred.

United-Crash-Claims
Lives of Rabbi, Wife

Rabbi Kenneth Berger, former leader of a Greenbelt congregation, and his wife were filled in the United Airlines disaster in Sioux City, Iowa, last week.

Editorial

Chapter Fifteen:
Departed Too Young

As dictated by Jewish tradition, Uncle Kenny's and Aunt Aviva's funerals had to take place within forty-eight hours of their bodies returning to Philadelphia. Of course, Dad missed it because he was maintaining his hospital bedside vigil for Avi in Iowa. I never knew whether missing his brother's funeral weighed heavily upon Dad's heart for the rest of his life.

I realized at Uncle Kenny's funeral just how revered he was as a rabbi. To me, he'd always been Uncle Kenny, but to Jewish communities around the world, he was Rabbi Kenneth Berger. Rabbis from every corner of the globe called to offer condolences and pay their respects.

My aunt and uncle's funeral was standing room only—not one seat left empty—with people crowding the aisles and pushing in through the doors. I wished more than anything my dad could have been there to see his dearest brother honored in such a wonderful way. Local news stations called my mom to record the funeral, but she always said no. It was not a place for entertainment.

So many people attended the funeral that, to avoid utter chaos, the Montgomery County Police Department blocked off all side streets for the journey from the funeral home to the cemetery, allowing the procession to make way without interruption. The route wound through Southampton to Bethayres to Meadowbrook to Huntingdon Valley to Philadelphia, lined the entire way with police cars stopping all traffic. It was fascinating to see.

In all, around 600 people attended. Only two places in Philly host Jewish funerals, and we had chosen Goldstein's Funeral Home. The directors told us later it was the single biggest funeral they'd ever organized. It was only eclipsed by my dad's, which was to come ten years later.

The service was solemn, but not without its fair share of drama. We left the funeral home and, in a long precession, headed to the cemetery. The day was warm, sun shining upon the vast gathering who crowded between the gravestones to say their final goodbyes to my aunt and uncle. Wearing an all-black mourning dress, I was uncomfortable and felt as if I was about to overheat—and looking at the reddened faces around me, I knew I wasn't the only one.

Aunt Aviva's mom, a stern Israeli lady who didn't speak a word of English, quietly sobbed by the graveside throughout the ceremony, but as Aviva's coffin was lowered into the ground, she began screaming and crying harder. Without warning and before anyone could stop her, the poor woman jumped on top of the casket as it made its final journey downward. I could barely believe what I was witnessing—absolutely horrifying, raw grief.

After the funeral, we headed back to our home, where everyone would gather to sit Shiva. For Jews, very little surpasses the solemnity of Shiva, which comes with its own set of rigidly observed rules. For seven days, we cannot leave our homes at all. There can be no work, shopping, parties, visiting with people—absolutely nothing at all, other than attending the synagogue for specific services to honor the deceased loved ones and bring comfort to family and close friends. So strict is this rule that, when I got married, the mother of a friend of mine had passed, and my friend was forced to miss my wedding.

We were also not allowed to cut our hair, had to cover all the mirrors in the house, and could only wear sneakers—shoes with leather soles were banned during the entire seven days. As a little kid learning the rules and regulations of my faith and culture, I was taught that during Shiva no one could be seen enjoying life. The ritual was meant to honor those who'd just lost theirs.

Outside the Shiva house stood a table with a pitcher of water and rolls of paper towels for everyone to wash their hands, to symbolize cleansing themselves of death and avoid bringing it into the home. Once they came in, all there was to sit on were incredibly uncomfortable hard little wooden stools. Back in Israel, apparently, those special little stools were the *only* chairs they had, which I could barely begin to imagine.

You see, Shiva is not about us or how we look or even how comfortable or bored we are. It's about giving over your time to contemplate and remember those who have passed. Inside the Shiva house, a special candle burns for the full seven days and, for the forty-eight hours prior to the burial, one is lit at the funeral home too. Tradition tells us this is to help light the way for the soul to see where it is going, just in case it has not transitioned to the afterlife.

Unconditional Love

For the duration of Shiva, since we weren't allowed out of the house to even go to the grocery store, it became tradition that friends and family would send food and dinners. They organized among themselves who would send what and when, and my family ate well throughout.

My uncle had once been a rabbi in Maryland, and members of his congregation rented a bus, which rolled up outside our house. It was packed solid with people who'd known him back then, who had travelled all the way to Philly to observe the seven-day mourning period with our family. Additionally, Uncle Kenny's Tampa congregation chartered an airplane and flew in. My aunt was from Israel and her mom, sister, and brother also stayed with us. My home was packed to the rafters with black-clad mourners and alive with a constant coming and going of people we'd never seen before, all united in grief.

Because so many people filled my house, I slept at my friend Julie's every night and left early in the morning. I was required home for Minyan—an important part of Shiva—so I had to be up *very* early on each of the seven days to make sure I arrived home by 7 a.m.

Unfortunately, though, it was forbidden to take any of the kindly donated food out of the house which meant, when I went to Julie's, I had to leave all those scrumptious dishes behind! I probably could have snuck something out had I wanted to, but such is the strength of my tradition and culture, the thought never even entered my head!

On a personal level, for twenty-one-year-old me, sitting Shiva was an arduous, boring task. All day, for seven long days, the house was quiet despite the constant influx of people, the atmosphere crushingly sad, and there was nothing to look forward to other than the Minyan service in the evening. People who knew my aunt and uncle well told stories about them to help make the time go by a little bit quicker. It felt good to have such sweet, positive vibes amid all the raw grief, to hear about Uncle Kenny and Aunt Aviva, and to have good people around. It's the most comforting part of the Shiva tradition.

But bored and craving social interaction, I soon discovered my own way of escaping the gloomy atmosphere. My friends came for Shiva, but always left just in time to make it into the city for a fun night of drinking! Although I couldn't go out with them, Julie never left my side, and we would go to the neighborhood TGI Fridays and get a drink. It was some relief, although we weren't having as much fun as our friends downtown. Sadly, though, not all my friends supported me; some even disappeared altogether during my time of need. Friends I'd gone out with all the time, lent money to for drinks, or gave them a ride because they didn't want to drink and drive—they were nowhere to be found.

After a few days of Shiva, I got a huge surprise when my friend Kim walked into my house. She had been in Israel, and I hadn't been able to share anything with her. Kim knew my family better than anyone, we'd been friends since second grade. I'd had no idea her trip to Israel had ended, and she was on her way back to Philadelphia. Her mom picked her up at the airport and drove her right to my house. I was so happy to see her and sat on the stairs at my parents' house just hugging her!

I guess it's times like those when we all find out who our real friends are! And I found out young. It was a helpful lesson to take with me for the rest of my life.

One night, Julie and I snuck out. My friend Billy lived in Meadowbrook Apartments, just a short drive around the corner from my parents' house, and I knew where he hid his front door key.

"Billy's out of town for the week. We can go get high—Billy always has a decent stash lying around," I told Julie with a sly grin as we made our way down the street. With all the people coming and going for Shiva, no one noticed us creep out.

We arrived at Billy's apartment, made ourselves comfortable on the couch, turned on the TV, and smoked some weed. We were ecstatic. We did the same thing again a few days in a row until one night we heard something at the door. Maybe a key? Perhaps we were too high and imagining things.

But no…

The key rattled in the lock and the door opened, while Julie and I slumped there wasted on the couch!

Who walked in? None other than two old friends from high school who also happened to know that Billy was away and where he hid his key.

I exchanged glances with Julie. Part of me knew we'd just gotten caught at Billy's, but these guys were doing the exact same thing. Who was going to tell him?

We stayed at Billy's until the small hours of the following morning, getting high with those two guys. After that, I went over to Billy's every night after Shiva. Usually, he wasn't there, and Julie would go with me. One night, we smoked opium. I have no idea where we got it. It kind of looked like Neutrogena soap—sort of a translucent, goldish color. That high led to some deep conversations and thoughts about the plane crash. It drove me a little crazy and exacerbated my visions of the crash, the fire, the burning people, and those terrible screams. I became incredibly emotional and cried most of the night. Julie never left my side and was always there for me.

One thing the crash helped me realize, though, was that life really is too short to waste on dumb things and even dumber people. Life is for *living*, and I'd gained a newfound enthusiasm to make the very most of every single day I had.

There was one detail of the mourning process I thought was meaningful, one I experienced firsthand some years later. When you were the person who had lost someone close—a parent, grandparent, sibling, spouse—you were given a small pin with a black ribbon, which was ceremonially ripped in front of a rabbi and the pin worn directly over the heart. The significance was clear: your heart was broken at the loss of your loved one.

In Israel, instead of a pin, they ripped their clothes and didn't change out of them for the whole seven days of Shiva. I was pleased we didn't observe that tradition in my house. The many people who visited from Israel did and, to be honest, they kind of smelled by the end of the week.

Although Dad was in Iowa, he still worked his magic to ensure the family was well taken care of and things ran smoothly at home and with his business. Our house was so busy and filled with so many mourners, our street was in danger of clogging up since there were no sidewalks. We lived right across from Lorimer Park, which had a parking lot about a mile from our house. My parents got the idea for Dad's workers to ferry people to and from the parking lot down the road, creating a valet service to drive the cars back and forth between my house and the park parking lot. In his absence, Dad arranged for his foreman Tim to organize the transportation of mourners. He was paid handsomely for his hard work.

It was an incredibly difficult time for me in so many ways. The crash and its aftermath seemed so tragically surreal—losing beloved family members in such an awful way was painful beyond comprehension. Seeing the effect, it had on Dad hurt me even more. He'd not only lost his brother, but he'd also missed out on saying goodbye because of his staunch sense of duty and determination to stay by Avi's bedside until she recovered from her coma. Seeing Dad in so much pain and not having him home for the funeral only added to the profound sense of sadness and loss hanging over me.

But above everything else happening, it was my relationship with G-d that most confused and angered me. I was only twenty-one and had always enjoyed a healthy relationship with G-d. We weren't an overly devout family, but we observed all the Jewish traditions and delighted in the togetherness of the various holidays.

A few years before the crash, I started questioning my formerly unwavering belief in G-d when Aunt Aviva bravely fought a fierce battle against breast cancer. She underwent a double mastectomy and grueling chemotherapy, yet her own belief in G-d remained steadfast throughout—I guess being a rabbi's wife helped. Also, my uncle *was a rabbi*. And the two of them were up there in the clouds with G-d, only to die, crushed to death, in an airplane crash.

What kind of G-d puts a person through an ordeal like cancer only to cut down their life so shortly after they've beaten the disease and are looking forward to so many more years raising their young children and loving their family and friends?

Unconditional Love

The question has stayed with me from those dark days to now. Although I did finally make my peace with G-d, I can honestly say our relationship was never the same after my uncle and aunt died. I still dearly love the rich culture and tradition my Jewish faith affords me, but that's as far as it goes nowadays.

While mourning, I also became painfully aware of the fact I seemed to be the only one who was expected to help. Thinking back, I was the one person who ferried visitors, organized stuff, and supported my parents—my sisters rarely contributed.

It finally dawned on me just how much my family leaned on me and *expected* me to step up whenever something needed doing. I knew nothing different—I always embraced my older sister role without question. So, it was me who joined my grandfather at the cemetery and funeral home to ensure the double funeral went smoothly. Pop-pop was understandably distraught at the loss of his son and beloved daughter-in-law, although he maintained an air of dignity throughout that made me love and admire him even more. I greeted people, helped set up the coat rack my mom rented, and met the local charity reps to hand over the food we couldn't finish. While you weren't allowed to take food from a Shiva house, you were permitted to donate it to charity. Also, I drove my aunt's family back and forth from their hotel a half hour away. I always checked on my mom to make sure she was eating, and I tended to all those people in our home. I felt it was my duty to make sure everyone and everything was okay, especially with my dad away by my cousin's bedside.

Ilana, who was on her way to our house from camp, was terribly allergic to dogs, which didn't bode well for our family German Shepherd Chance who was placed in a kennel until they decided what to do. I had grown up with German Shepherds. My parents had built a fenced outdoor area, the "pen," complete with a concrete floor, for the dog to use to go to the bathroom. But the pen wasn't going to help with Ilana's allergy.

Sadly, Chance had a stroke in the kennel and died just a week after the crash. My sister Tammy was devastated. "Everybody is dying!" she wailed when Mom broke the news of our beloved dog's passing, and I think our entire heartbroken family felt the same. While I was upset, I wasn't the biggest dog lover at the time, and Chance's death didn't seem like anything to me compared to the trauma of losing my uncle's family.

Uncle Kenny had lived a rabbi's lifestyle, which, while comfortable, was nowhere near what we were used to. We lived in a bigger beautiful home with a pool, drove expensive cars, and wore designer clothes. With Avi and Jonathan still in the hospital in Iowa, Ilana struggled to settle in at Mom and Dad's house.

My heart went out to her: she had found herself suddenly all alone in a strange house in a strange city, with no one to comfort her. It was easy to see she was incredibly uncomfortable with the whole situation. Who wouldn't be?

Dad and Jonathan were left to make their own way back to Philly. Jonathan could not get back on a plane—understandable—and so my dad traveled with him from Iowa to Philadelphia by train. Out of the relationships he'd forged with the nurses and hospital staff, Dad chose one of his favorite nurses to join them on the trip back to Philly. I mean, who would do that? Dad had that effect on people, and I'm sure the money he offered helped. He'd probably paid the pretty nurse handsomely for her time and inconvenience—although, such was Dad's charisma, I can imagine she would have gladly tagged along for free! Rather sweetly, she remained in touch with our family over the years.

Eventually, Avi awoke from her coma and recovered enough to be transferred from the hospital in Iowa by medical airplane to the world-famous Magee Rehabilitation Hospital in Philly—one of the very best in the country—thanks to my parents. Even though she was awake, she remained bedridden and required a heck of a lot of physical therapy to get back to anywhere close to normal. She had extensive physical damage, and nobody was sure what her mental condition was; she had to learn how to walk and speak all over again. Her full recovery today from that dreadful accident is nothing short of miraculous.

In the years to follow, back in Tampa, my uncle's community named its post-b'nai mitzvah community program "Berger High School" in his memory, which reinforced Kenny's family legacy and helped keep the name alive long after his death. His congregation also set up a fund at the Tampa Orlando Pinellas Jewish Foundation to carry on the Berger family's leadership presence.

Chapter Sixteen:
1989—The Aftermath

If we have built on the fragile cornerstones of human wisdom, pride, and conditional love, things may look good for a while, but a weak foundation causes collapse when storms hit.

—Charles Stanley

In February 1989, five months before the plane crash, Uncle Sammy married his wife, Aunt Tris. My family traveled to San Diego for the exciting wedding weekend. None of us knew it would be the last time our family would all be together, truly happy and carefree.

So, Uncle Sammy and Aunt Tris were newlyweds at the time of the crash. She had moved across the country from San Diego to be with him, and both had successful careers working in New York City at the time of the crash.

Nevertheless, from my understanding, my parents told Sammy in no uncertain terms he *had* to move to Philadelphia to be close by to help with Avi while she was still at Magee Hospital. They reminded him he owed them a debt of gratitude big enough to warrant him uprooting his new bride again and leaving behind the life he'd built in NYC to help in Philly.

Uncle Sammy was the baby of my father's family. He was nine years old when my parents married, and only eleven years older than me! My dad had acted more like a father to Sammy than an older brother and had always taken good care of him. Sometimes, I think of Dad like some mafia guy: *kiss my ring and you owe me forever*. Such was the energy he exuded.

Unconditional Love

Uncle Sammy indeed left New York to move to Philadelphia. He and Tris found a place close to the Magee Hospital, and once they were firmly ensconced in Philly, my parents informed them it was *their* job to take care of Avi.

What depresses me, looking back on everything, is my sisters, my parents, and me rarely visited Avi in the hospital. It was my grandparents' responsibility to handle that, and something my uncle and new aunt took *very* seriously too. They called on Avi all throughout her stay at Magee.

At home, at first, everything appeared peachy. Jonathan healed well from his physical injuries—of course, it was impossible at such an early stage to tell how he was coping with the psychological trauma of surviving a horrific plane crash that cost his parents' lives. Ilana seemed to be okay too, but she must have been so uncomfortable living in an unfamiliar house without her parents or older sister.

We doubled up in our bedrooms, so everyone had a place to sleep. The cot from the basement was brought into my room and placed directly next to my bed. That was the only way it would fit; there was little space to walk anywhere else in my room. But I was so excited to share my room with Jonathan. Lisa had a trundle bed, which allowed someone to sleep in her room too.

Construction soon began to build three new bedrooms on the other side of the house, just off the den. My and my sisters' rooms were right down the hall from our parents. My cousins would each get one of our old bedrooms, while my sisters and me would get the new rooms. That way, my cousins were closer to my parents. A circular staircase, which was very cool back then, would be the focus of the new addition, with the bedrooms placed off each of the three floors. On the bottom floor was a bedroom and full-size bathroom for my sister. My room was on the main floor, right off the den. Up the circular staircase on the top floor, my other sister occupied the third.

Outwardly, my cousins appeared okay and seemed to get on with their new life—kids are nothing if not adaptable—but I often caught flashes of despair in their eyes when they thought no one was looking. I guess it was their way of coping—using their stiff upper lips and muddling through one day at a time—and I knew they wouldn't wish to appear ungrateful for my parents' hospitality. They sucked it up and put on brave faces.

I found it peculiar when, straight away, Jonathan and Ilana began calling my parents Mom and Dad—literally, from the minute they began living under our roof. It sounded weird, and I couldn't help but wonder if it had come from my poor cousins desperately needing to replace the parents they'd so tragically lost or from my own parents. Home videos from black-tie affairs show Jonathan calling my parents Mom and Dad. It didn't seem right to me. It was like they were forgetting their own parents too quickly. My parents were their *aunt* and *uncle*, not mom and dad.

My parents provided my cousins with a wholly different lifestyle than the one they'd been used to. A rabbi's salary was nowhere close to the kind of money at our disposal. But it seemed my dad wanted, more than anything, to make my mom happy—over and above even his fierce loyalty toward his family.

From the moment Mom had walked into my bedroom to break the news about the crash, I'd noticed a distinct shift in her demeanor, a dark *disappointment* in her eyes. I reckoned she knew even then how much her life was about to change. Before, nothing like this had figured into her plans for her future with my dad. I understood how the tragedy had been a huge disappointment, but my parents had always raised me to believe family came first and foremost. As much as the crash and its aftermath disrupted Mom, she remained a strong woman. Dad continued with his normal work routine, and Mom stayed busy at home, sending my cousins to school.

Dad constantly tried to make things easier for her. He employed a chef caterer to make dinner for us every day. He also tried to hire the husband of our housekeeper Joan to chauffeur the kids. He even offered to let Joan, and her husband live with us to help more, but they declined. Joan would become my rock, though; she saw everything, knew everything, and treated me like her granddaughter. She ended up being the one person with whom I could confide my true feelings about my family.

Despite all his effort, my mom just wasn't happy. She didn't seem to love my cousins, and it must have been difficult for her to grapple with that feeling. Her inner strength compelled her to take the necessary care of my cousins, but her heart wasn't in it at all. Dad only wanted to contribute by hiring anyone he could to take some of the responsibilities off her plate.

From the beginning, Mom was concerned with my cousins' weight. At the time, I still believed everything she said—after all, it was how she'd raised me—and supported her insistence they needed to lose weight. Remember, I had grown up being told I needed to always retain an ideal body shape. If I got even the slightest bit pudgy, it would be brought to my attention immediately. My mom constantly repeated her mantra: "If I thought you were happy being heavy, I'd let you stay that way." She knew I wasn't glad to be "heavy"—after all, she had conditioned me not to be.

Mom was a gorgeous woman and often told me, "Being beautiful can be painful." My parents were obsessed with my appearance and would stop at nothing to make sure we always maintained the air of absolute perfection. I almost felt like I was on show, especially when we went out for dinner, like some trophy child.

It didn't help either that my mom considered Jonathan overweight. Bear in mind he was eight and only wanted to eat bologna and Doritos. My mother would have none of that! I don't know if she hated the way fat looked or viewed it as a blatant illustration of excess and lack of self-control when appearances and what people thought were paramount to her.

Regardless, Mom put Jonathan on a strict diet. I wasn't living at home and didn't know how he reacted to his new diet on a day-to-day basis. But when he lost weight, he was thrilled about how he looked! Of course, his reaction only validated my mom's behavior—the boy was happier when he was skinnier!

When my own son turned eight, he was heavy himself. I had no desire to obsess overweight like my parents had. I just wanted him to be happy. He was only a child, and I didn't plan to instill issues with food at such a tender age, like Mom and Dad did to me. I suggested healthy options at mealtimes, but didn't force them; he always had options. I believed that, when he was old enough, he could decide what size he liked best for himself. To be honest, he probably wishes I had been stricter instead of doing the exact opposite of what my parents had done. Sure enough, when he grew up, he decided he didn't enjoy being heavy and lost some weight. Of course, I loved him no matter his size.

When my son turned eight, all these revelations upset and infuriated me. If, G-d forbid, my mom, sisters, or anybody else for that matter had to take care of my boy because I'd been killed in a plane crash, it sickened me to imagine anybody would even *think* about having an issue with his weight!

I used to drive a little girl to Hebrew School every week, and she was so chubby she didn't really fit in the car seat. I looked at her and thought, if I had to take her in because something happened to her parents, I wouldn't even care about her weight. In fact, I would kiss her fat belly and love every minute of it.

I was confused. I agreed with my mom that Jonathan shouldn't eat bologna and Doritos for every meal. But now, as a mother myself, I know I would have given my poor cousin as much bologna and as many Doritos as he wished. The kid had just lost his parents, was living in a strange home with aunts, uncles, and cousins he didn't know well, and his big sister was still in the hospital. Who could possibly care about his weight?

My parents also expected my grandparents to help with my cousins. Unfortunately, they weren't contributing as much as Mom and Dad needed them to, and this led to resentment, anger, fights, and ultimately, a broken family.

My father wasn't blind to what was going on in his own home and with Mom. He understood she was overwhelmed by the additional responsibility he'd heaped on top of her because of the commitment *he'd* made to his brother and family. I don't know if Mom even had any say in it or if she'd just been expected to suck it up and accept her new life. From day one, my dad agreed to take the kids and would hear no arguments from anybody—Mom included. And, as Dad worked most of the time, Mom was left to raise his brother's children, while his parents and brother weren't aiding her.

I was only twenty-one and hardly wise to the world, but I watched everything begin to snowball once my parents realized no one else was meeting their exacting expectations. My uncle, aunt, and grandparents were not doing "enough," which only built into bitter resentment as time went on.

I believed what my parents told me about nobody assisting them enough with my cousins. Over and over, my parents reiterated how they had supported my grandparents for years and years, so they didn't have to work. My parents owned their house, put my grandparents on the company payroll, and were always there for anything they needed. They also explained how they had provided for Uncle Sammy throughout high school and college, gifting him money for every A he received and buying him his first car. My mom and dad believed they'd always taken care of my grandparents and my uncle, but they weren't stepping up and repaying that support when we needed it most.

However, when Jonathan played Little League baseball, Pop-pop drove him to and from some of his games to help Mom. But that still wasn't enough: Pop-pop *had* to commit to taking my cousin to every game. According to my parents, it was the very least he could do. Pop-pop enjoyed spending the time with his grandson, but my mother maintained it just wasn't enough. Don't forget, Mom-mom and Pop-pop had just lost their son and daughter-in-law. They were grieving too. But nobody, not even me, recognized that.

And it wasn't just my grandparents. Dad's first cousins were expected to chip in too. Some of my friends' parents were also asked to organize playdates for their kids and my cousins. As with most tragedies, everybody was so passionate to help at the beginning, only to forget a couple months later. People move on with their lives and good intentions fade away.

Remember, I wasn't living at home anymore, but from what I saw, almost every relationship within my father's family was breaking down. *Nobody was helping enough.* That's all I heard, repeatedly.

Once Avi was discharged from Magee, she lived with Uncle Sammy and Tris. They did everything they could to make her feel at home and heal her from her physical and emotional trauma, all while working full-time at their new careers. One day, my dad found out my uncle was leaving Avi with a nanny so he and his new bride could go to work, and he went ballistic. How could they leave her with a nanny?

Something had to give. There was only so much two people could do in such circumstances. But my dad empathized with their struggle and confronted my uncle. I wasn't present for the argument, but I could imagine it.

Unconditional Love

"What do you mean you're paying for a nanny?" My dad was absolutely red-in-the-face livid!

"We did what we thought was best for Avi," Uncle Sammy told him. "For when Tris and I can't be here for her."

"This is totally unacceptable, Sammy!" Dad raised his voice louder. "It's your responsibility to take care of Avi, not some… some *stranger*!"

My poor cousin was right there in my uncle's living room, party to the escalating row. It was the very last thing she needed to hear after everything she'd gone through.

But it didn't matter what he said. Uncle Sammy could tell when he was beaten. He knew his older brother well enough to be sure he'd never back down—*ever*. As he'd shown time and time again, it simply wasn't in my dad's nature to give up on getting his own way.

Sammy told him, "Me and Tris have to rebuild our lives here because you insisted, we move to Philadelphia, and we need our—"

Before he could say *independence*, my dad cut him off. "You owe me, Sammy. I've taken good care of you over the years. All I'm asking is for you to look after Avi. And this is how you repay me."

"We *are* taking care of her—that's precisely why we hired the nanny." Uncle Sammy's protest fell on deaf ears.

"Family takes care of family," Dad said softly. "And if you're not prepared to do the job properly and take your responsibility seriously, I'm taking Avi home with me."

And with that, Dad instructed my cousin to pack up her things right then and there and make her way out to his car.

Whatever Uncle Sammy said next to my dad, he didn't hear it. Dad had made up his mind, and my cousin was on her way to live with him and Mom. That's the story according to my parents, at least. Who knows how real it is?

On a positive note, Avi would be once again living with her brother and sister. Her return made for a bittersweet family reunion.

The fallout was inevitable after Dad took Avi away. Relations soured with Uncle Sammy, and as result, with my grandparents as well. Tensions strained between my parents and Dad's family.

My mom worked diligently to enroll Avi into Abington Friends Private School, only ten minutes away from the house. She wasn't fully caught up, but her recovery so far was miraculous, and mom didn't want to send her to a "special" school. She met with various staff and agreed to provide Avi with permanent tutors in all subjects. Mom made sure Avi was in the best place possible to excel, meet friends, and succeed. It appeared as if my parents were 100% committed to raising my cousins and giving them a beautiful life.

Unfortunately, that wasn't the way things turned out.

A funny memory from immediately after the crash was when one day, I was home, sitting in my room, and the phone rang. I answered to what I thought was my friend Andy pulling a prank.

"Hello?"

A deep, deep voice replied, "Hello. Is Jonathan there?" I asked who was calling, and he said, "This is Hulk Hogan."

Yeah, right.

Laughing, I said, "Andy, I know it's you!"

"No, this is really Hulk Hogan."

We went back and forth a couple times until I realized it wasn't Andy. It was *really* Hulk Hogan.

A certain group of athletes and sports players support children in times of tragedy, such as the plane crash. Hulk Hogan was calling my cousin to offer backstage tickets to his next wrestling match in Philadelphia. How amazing! My cousins also received an autographed ball from Daryl Strawberry and a signed jersey from the quarterback of the Miami Dolphins, Dan Marino, if memory serves. I wonder where those things are today.

Chapter Seventeen:
Another Cruise Already

There is no going back but there is accepting your new normal.
—Jay Crownover

In December 1989, five months after the crash that killed their parents and almost killed Jonathon and Avi, my three cousins embarked on an airplane to Florida to catch the cruise ship for our Caribbean Christmas vacation. How those kids managed to summon up the necessary fortitude, I'll never know!

I think their bravery had a lot to do with my parents, whose philosophy had always been "Get right back on the horse." Mom and Dad explained to my cousins that the sooner they got back on a plane, the better. Face the fear.

I also realize now that my parents had already planned and paid for the cruise and weren't going to miss it because of the tragedy—even though Avi was still very broken, using a wheelchair most of the time and wearing ankle braces. Thinking about it now, how *could* Avi go on a cruise? Really?

By then, Jonathan and I had formed a special relationship. He was the little brother I'd never had, and I treasured the bond we forged during those difficult times. We became even closer after sharing my room, and I loved spending time with him. On the flight to Florida, Jonathan *insisted* upon sitting next to me. It was the *only* way he'd get on the plane!

My parents' special friends Jacob and Martine, as well as their three girls, were flying from Paris to meet us on the cruise and complete the ensemble. Despite the horrific events of that year, it felt good to have everyone together in a happy place. It was, in many ways, just like old times. Dad fell into his old, familiar role of taking care of everyone—and insisting we do *everything* together—and made it his job to direct the menu from the moment we set foot on board the ship.

Dad also wished for Jacob and Martine to sit close to our table at dinner. However, on the first night, he was annoyed to discover his request had not been followed. Upset, he ordered the captain to move them to a table right next to ours, as he had already demanded. The captain replied he couldn't that night; it was too late, and all the tables were already set up. Well, that was not an acceptable answer. After explaining Jacob and Martine had come all the way from Paris and that he'd already asked for them to be seated nearby, he realized nobody was listening. So, he started moving chairs and tables around the dining room himself to place his dear friends and their daughters adjacent to us—much to the amusement of the other diners! But he clearly wasn't laughing. The captain told Dad to stop, but he didn't. He'd lost his temper and had decided if nobody was going to help him, he would do it himself.

My mother spent much of the vacation on her own in her cabin. She was depressed and had brought along her resentment and bitterness at the sudden unwelcome disruption to her life. I had never seen my mom act like that in my whole life.

Jacob and Martine validated her feelings by saying that these kids just don't fit into your family. Words that my mom would hang on to and live by.

On the other hand, Dad was delighted to be with his kids, including the newest three of the bunch. I have a picture of Dad on Jet Skis with Jonathan, both grinning wide. Unlike Mom, he'd welcomed the cousins into his family in a heartbeat and treated them the same as he'd treated us growing up. I felt for him throughout the cruise, though, because it was obvious he wanted his wife to be happy too.

Although she preferred to be alone, Mom's influence permeated beyond her cabin. Her obsession with *all* her family looking perfect at *all* times meant she imposed a strict dress code on my cousins. Because Avi and Ilana were not thin, and maybe a little chubby, she forced them to wear cover-ups over their bathing suits by the pool, while my sisters and I were allowed to show off our nice bodies.

To this day, Ilana hates Mom for how she treated her: the dieting, the hallway posture training, and all the unfamiliar expectations. All of it was completely alien to my cousin, a regime imposed upon her by the family who had taken her in. It made her incredibly unhappy.

Unconditional Love

Star Princess

Chapter Eighteen:
Off to Law School

The plane crash upended all our lives. It disrupted my plans for law school in Boston, where I was supposed to move in the next couple months. I didn't want to be so far away from home and decided I couldn't go. I had to stay nearby and help my mom with my cousins, so I settled for Widener Law School in Delaware. I couldn't be too upset at the change because, after all, I still had my family, unlike my poor cousins.

Widener was an "insurance" school for me, and I had already applied and been accepted. I called the dean of the school, Dean Santoro—I will never forget his name—one day in the dining room at my parents' house. I informed him my loved ones had been in the recent United Airlines crash, explaining how my aunt and uncle had passed away and my badly injured cousins were coming to live with my family. I also let him know I had already been accepted to Widener Law School but had planned to study at a different university in Boston. I asked if he would still honor my acceptance because I wanted to stay home and help my parents take care of my cousins.

Much to my shock and amazement, he said, "No."

What?

I asked if he could just put an extra chair in the classroom for me, and he again said, "No."

I couldn't believe his absolute lack of empathy. How often did someone call with a tragedy such as ours? When I hung up the phone, I was distraught and in tears. I knew Dad would have to get involved.

Unconditional Love

From what I understand, Dad either called or met with Dean Santoro, he never elaborated. Another secret I dared ask about. But the result was I could attend Widener's new Harrisburg campus but not the main one in Delaware. That was the deal my dad struck, and that's precisely what I did.

It felt amazing to finally head off to law school and find some respite from the relentless doom and gloom back home. But on some level, I also felt like I was abandoning my family—especially my parents because the full weight of the aftermath of the crash seemed to press down on their shoulders. They tried their best to hide the profound sadness of the loss suffered and the three new children to raise. Still, we all saw how depressed my mom had become at having to cope with instant trio. Her despondence put even more stress on my dad, and he did everything he could to make the situation easier for her. As hard as she tried, I'm sure my poor cousins were under no illusion as to how much of a burden their presence was to her.

Shortly before I went to law school, I watched the old Pacino movie "*And Justice for All*', which shows how difficult it is to stay in law school. The scene where the professor tells the lecture hall filled with eager, fresh students to "Look to the left, look to the right," and explains how one of the students on either side won't make it through the first semester was especially poignant to me. But rather than dampening my spirits, it hardened my resolve to not only graduate but to study harder and do the best I could.

Wrapped up in working damned hard to attain the A and B grades my parents expected of me, I was never fully aware of how bad relations were becoming back home among Dad, my grandparents, and Uncle Sammy, who had just upturned his entire life and relocated with his new wife all the way from New York to Philadelphia.

Because I had chosen to go to law closer to home to help my mom with my cousins, I visited home as often as I could to help, treating my cousins to the movies, bowling, or anything else they enjoyed—partly to give Mom a break and partly to give those poor kids some kind of normality in their wrecked lives. Looking back, it seems my actions were more like obligations—or at least, I think that was the way my cousins must have felt. But I *really* wanted to be there for them. I was still in my early twenties, but I felt both a responsibility and a desire to lend a hand. Sadly, it all felt too fake. Maybe that was true, and I was trying *too hard*, only making things worse for my poor cousin. Nonetheless, I felt I was doing my very best in a dark time.

My sister did go to Boston for college, which was too far for her to keep popping back home, so she didn't feel the same accountability. Also, I felt like my duty was "assumed." No one suggested that I still go to Boston for law school, or ever actually requested I stay closer to home—it was what was going to happen.

Unconditional Love

After my first year of law school—a very successful year, I must add, in which I finished with a 3.25 GPA—I had to undergo gynecological surgery. Since it was major surgery, I was forced to take six full weeks of bed rest. I recovered at my parents' home and became all too aware of the deteriorating situation between them and my dad's family. I experienced what it was like for my cousins to live in our house, and I felt isolated from them. They never came down to my new room on the other side of the house to spend time with me. In fact, I overheard one of my cousins on the phone with a friend say I was just faking my illness! The tension was palpable and uncomfortable. The love and laughter I remembered so well had disappeared. I also began to realize the enormity of the impact the crash had had upon my family—in particular, the effect having to look after my cousins and the subsequent fallout had upon my mom.

Under normal circumstances, my grandparents would have visited me in the hospital. They'd bring flowers, candy, books, and magazines and stay as long as possible to chat and keep me company. But…

They didn't.

Not even *once*.

I didn't even talk to them the night before I went in. I called Pop-pop and Mom-mom from the hospital waiting room and managed to get ahold of them right before the doctors took me back for surgery. It was completely out of the ordinary, and I was confused by everything going on around me.

Things were different, that much was painfully clear. The drastic change to my once loving family was impossible to ignore, and the whole thing baffled and upset me.

During my bed rest, about a week after I got home, Pop-pop and Mom-mom finally came to see me. I was hurt and angry and told them so.

Pop-pop made a whole bunch of lame excuses as to why they'd avoided the hospital. He even showed me his calendar so he could point out all the things they'd *had* to do instead of coming to see me. My grandparents only lived fifteen minutes away from my parents. Sure, on paper, it looked like they'd been busy, but I didn't believe for one minute they'd been too booked to find the time to visit their granddaughter for a whole week after she'd had major surgery.

What made their actions—or lack thereof—even harder for me to accept was the fact that, throughout my entire childhood, I'd been so close to Mom-mom and Pop-pop. From junior high to high school, they'd come to all the football and basketball games I'd cheered at and every graduation and had even traveled to Washington D.C. to visit me at college. All my friends knew them; they'd been a huge part of my life. Based on how nurturing they'd been when I was growing up, I couldn't imagine not having them there to support and comfort me in my time of need.

With that experience, I could *really* feel the weird shift in my formerly close, happy family dynamic. It also urged me to view them all and how I'd been raised with different, often critical eyes.

Dad worked practically all the time, and my mom basically raised the trio all on her own, but remember we also had a chef, a maid, drivers, and a healthy bank account. They could easily have hired a full-time nanny or anyone else to lessen Mom's responsibilities. Unlike Mom, Dad welcomed the new kids into his home—and his big heart—with open arms and treated all three like his own. Of course, Jonathan was the son he'd always wanted, which made him extra special.

Unfortunately, I wasn't spared my parents' vitriol.

"Nobody helps us."

"After everything we've done to help them, they all just left us to it after the crash."

"We paid for everything!"

"Your grandparents wouldn't be living in that house if we hadn't bought it for them."

"We've had them on our payroll for years and have been supporting them forever."

"And, as for Sammy—I'd have expected more gratitude from him and his wife, considering we gave so much to him over the years."

I believed *everything* my parents said. I felt so bad for them as they complained about how much they had done for my grandparents and my uncle. In my head, it was almost like a mafia movie—*I do something for you, you owe me.* That's kind of what I thought my dad was—something akin to a Jewish mob boss.

I will help you, but then you owe me.

My parents' disappointment toward the family rubbed off on me. More and more, the sentiment that everyone had abandoned my mom and dad to pick up the pieces following my aunt and uncle's deaths crept up on me. Because I was so close to my parents, I believed everything they said and their anger toward everyone transferred to me. It wasn't long before I, too, came to resent my grandparents and uncle for not helping and leaving my parents to do everything.

It was the summer of 1990, a year after the crash, and straight after I'd recovered from my surgery, I met Jon—the man who would become my husband. It had been my first night out after all the forced bed rest and the painful recuperation, and I was determined to have some fun with my friends. I'd not once imagined I'd meet my future spouse!

Chapter Nineteen:
Dating and Doctors

Jon was two years older than me and from Cheltenham, the high school right next to mine where the kids were more experienced with alcohol, drugs, and sex. It turned out we had something in common even before we met: his little sister, Missy Waxman, was one of the mean girls from Cheltenham. It seemed most Cheltenham girls were rude, nasty, sometimes just plain evil, and loved nothing more than to bully Abingdon girls. I believe they saw us as soft, naïve, easy targets.

My friends and I had a tradition of going to TGI Fridays on City Line Ave on Wednesday nights. Every Wednesday, the line to get in stretched all the way out the door. My friends and I figured out that, if we got there early to eat dinner, we would have a table and be able to stay all night! No waiting in line *and* prime table location for the whole evening!

It was at Fridays, on a Wednesday night, when I first met Jon. I told my friends I'd find someone with pot because we didn't have any. It was Andy's birthday, and we needed to get some weed!

"Hey, I *really* want to get high tonight," I told Jon barely five minutes into our conversation. I figured he'd be used to girls being more streetwise and direct than I typically was, so that's how I tried to act.

"You have pot?" Jon asked with a smirk. He knew damn well a sweet, well-to-do twenty-two-year-old Jewish girl like me would never be out and about with pot on her person.

I shook my head. "I have money, though. If *you* know where we can get some."

"I know where we can get some, all right." Jon smiled and patted his back pocket. His stash was in his jacket, but I think he wanted to emphasize his ass in a clumsy attempt to flirt with me.

It worked, and I blushed. "We can go to my friend's house to hang out and get high," I suggested. "Andy's cool, and he's got the house to himself this week." Andy's mom worked away from home for three weeks at a time, which meant he had free rein for most of the month.

Jon agreed and asked if he could bring his best friend Rob.

"Sure," I replied. "Why not?" I was excited, not because I liked Jon. I just wanted to get high.

Thus, off we went to Andy's house. So, Jon would know where to go, I rode shotgun in his car while Rob sat in the back. Not once did I think it was foolish or dangerous to ride in a car with a couple of guys I'd only just met. Times were so much more innocent back then.

We had a blast! Andy was as welcoming as usual. A couple of his friends were staying over, so we all got high together. As the night progressed, I developed feelings for Jon, and we kissed for hours on Andy's couch. Andy passed out on the floor of his mom's bedroom, so he wasn't going to be getting up any time soon.

But…

I knew my dad left for work every morning at 6.00 a.m. on the dot—he was an incredibly punctual man! That meant I had to be home *before* six, so he didn't realize I'd been out all night. If he did, I'd have to deal with his disapproval, even though I was an adult and had been living away from home at college!

Still a little stoned, Jon bundled me into his black Supra and hightailed it across town to get me home at 5:30. We said a quick goodbye, and I snuck back into the house as dawn crept across Philadelphia. Narrowly avoiding Dad, who was already up and about doing his morning ablutions, I jumped into bed and slept until almost noon.

Jon called me that afternoon and asked to see me again. We met up thirty-one nights in a row, even if it was late after he finished work, until I had to go back to law school.

***

I returned to law school in the fall of 1990, but quickly got sick again with the same problems I'd had before. Unfortunately, that meant having to undergo the same surgical procedure all over again. Too ill to continue studying and facing yet another six weeks or more of bed rest, I had no other option than to drop out of law school. And since the *whole* grade was based on the final exam, I received absolutely no credit whatsoever for all my hard work up until that point! That was the hardest part—all the work I had completed was worth absolutely nothing.

In November, I had the surgery and was forced to take it easy in bed. My grandparents repeated their odd behavior. Family tensions at home had not gotten any easier. I was further devastated to learn that, come February 1991, I would have to have the same surgery a *third* time!

I didn't like my doctor, Dr. Sedlacek, and not just because he kept delivering bad news or failed to fix my medical problem the first time around. He was one of those snooty doctors with what I considered to be a bad attitude and lousy bedside manners. He had a particular way of making me feel stupid and bothersome for asking questions about what was going on with my own body.

As a result, Mom didn't let Dr. Sedlacek perform a third surgery. Instead, she arranged for me to go to Sloan Kettering hospital in New York—the *very best* cancer hospital in the world! Sloan Kettering was a big teaching hospital that took in patients from all over the world: the rich, the famous, foreign dignitaries, and powerful politicians. Over half the patients there didn't speak any of English!

My doctor there was a wonderful, handsome African American man, Dr. Jones. He was the head of gyno-oncology and a prestigious physician. It helped that I loved the guy, and his bedside manner was a world apart from that of my previous doctor. I genuinely felt much more at ease with Dr. Jones and confident he was taking the very best care of me.

I had to attend appointments with Dr. Jones in New York every three months, and, as it transpired, I *didn't* have to have that third surgery at all. He performed several biopsies and was unable to find any "bad skin," which negated the need for more surgery.

Dr. Jones told me—yes, he took the time to patiently explain things, unlike my previous doctor! —that the first surgery hadn't removed all the cancer cells, and the second time around had left me "marginalized." That meant they'd keep a close eye on things but forgot to subject me to yet more operations. Finally, when I'd gotten the all-clear, I had plastic surgery to tidy things up a little. Sadly, there are not before and after pictures!

Through the entire ordeal, I had no choice but to witness firsthand my family become more and more fragmented and angry with each other. It was heartbreaking.

Except, I wasn't heartbroken. I was *furious*.

Chapter Twenty:
Physical Aggression

If you judge people, you have no time to love them.
—Mother Teresa

In the movies, it seems like everything turns out great and everyone becomes one happy family by pulling together through adversity. Unfortunately, that's not the way it went in *my* story. In fact, the whole family was fighting; I don't remember any love or laughter from that time, and things would never return to the way they were.

To make things worse, Ilana had begun hanging out with the stereotypical "kids from the wrong side of the tracks." It was '91 or '92, and word inevitably got back to Mom that Ilana was associating with the bad kids from the only black area of our nice suburban county, and she wasn't about to allow that to happen. She gave my poor cousin a whole "If you're living under my roof, you live by my rules" speech, which didn't go down that well with this teenager.

Teen rebellion and the fact she'd lost her parents aside, Ilana was acting out because she didn't want to live like our family. She considered us snobs who flaunted our money, and I bet she felt second-rate under my mom's constant scrutiny of her weight and appearance. (because I felt that way too!)

The courts had ordered videos to be recorded showing our lifestyle and the things my parents did for my cousins, such as vacations, camp, and the addition built onto the house. I never knew why and never asked.

Unconditional Love

Ilana carried on hanging out with her "bad" black friends, and Mom started researching boarding schools.

Boarding school?

My parents told me Ilana was dating black boys and getting into serious trouble, and that was why she had to move away. It wasn't until forty years later when I found out what Ilana believes is the truth. I was missing an integral part of the story. At that point, I was still brainwashed by my parents and didn't even think to question them sending my cousin off to boarding school.

What I didn't know was that Ilana had begged and begged my parents to let her live with our grandparents. It was obvious she wasn't happy at our house, and she told them she'd prefer to be with Mom-mom and Pop-pop. Jonathan also wanted to go with her; I don't think he was quite as miserable at my parents' house, but he was only ten and wanted to stay with his big sister. Neither of them had ever been comfortable in our home.

My grandparents were ecstatic at the idea; they were more than capable of taking care of their grandchildren. They even offered to let my cousin stay in the same school and drive her back and forth every day. They had nothing else to do and would have been glad to just have their beloved granddaughter with them.

But my parents outright refused to entertain the idea, even though my grandparents only lived fifteen minutes away from their house. To this day, I have no idea why my parents took the stance they did. I never knew about the option of going to my grandparents. More secrets. Years later, when I confronted my mom with this new information, she told me my cousin was lying to my face! She says there was never any discussion about my cousins living with my grandparents.

Throughout all this strife, Joan was a constant in my life. Our dear, loyal housekeeper was like a grandmother to me. She was my rock. She knew me just as well as my parents, if not more so. She saw things and listened to and knew everything going on in our house and within the family.

Before Ilana was packed off to boarding school, I was told the catalyst of the entire situation was Joan. I'm curious now how much disinformation my parents have subjected me to. I was told Joan had tattled to my mom about Ilana hanging around with the black kids in Crestmont—the most undesirable, roughest part of town. Crestmont was notorious back then for being a "bad area," and that piece of information resulted in Ilana being shipped off to boarding school.

However, Joan swears it wasn't true! She'd never once seen Ilana in Crestmont, nor had she heard *any* gossip to that effect. And she certainly hadn't said anything to my mother about it. Joan explained to me herself many years later how it wasn't her place to do so, even if she had known or seen something. So now I'm left trying to pick out which stories my parents told me were true and which ones weren't, and wondering how my heart really felt versus what my parents were saying and doing.

It was all messed up.

My parents also told me Jonathan begged me to go to school with Ilana. He was ten or eleven years old, and my parents claimed to tell him no. They said he *insisted* on going with his sister. The irony is that my parents did pack my two poor cousins off to boarding school, but didn't even send them to the same one so they could be with each other! Even more disgusting, I never went to visit either of them or neither did anyone else in my family. Those two kids were just sent away, right after losing their parents in such a tragic way.

They were children!

This event devastates me and keeps me up at night.

I was in law school at the time, but I can't use that as an excuse to not have been more involved. I was very uncomfortable with my dynamic with my parents—the ingrained belief they were *always* right, and I was *never* to disagree with them. We never discussed any of it as a family; whatever my parents wanted, that was what happened.

Mom and Dad remained steadfast to their bizarre decision to send both Ilana and Jonathan away to boarding schools—a long, long way from Philadelphia and too far for regular visits home to see their family. I never understood why. My parents could easily have afforded to pay an au pair to take care of my cousins at home, or even hire a nanny and a driver. But no, they were going to boarding school, and that was the end of it!

The night my cousins were to leave for boarding school is one of my most horrible, scary memories. I was there with Jon, my sisters, my cousins, Uncle Sammy and Tris, and my grandparents. Emotions ran high, and the atmosphere in my parents' house was frosty, to say the least.

Dad, Uncle Sammy, and Pop-pop had gone upstairs to my parents' bedroom to have some last-minute discussion about the plan to get the kids off to boarding school. All was quiet for some time, and I didn't think anything was unusual.

Suddenly, I heard an almighty crash, a yell of surprise and pain, and Uncle Sammy came flying down the stairs!

I shot up from the kitchen table and, to my shock, saw Pop-pop tumble down after him. Pop-pop stood at the bottom of the steps with Dad's gold chain clenched in one hand—he'd torn it clean off my dad's neck!

I wasn't allowed to go upstairs to see what had happened or find out if my dad was okay. My mom insisted on being the only one to go up. But I snuck up after her.

Dad was still in his bedroom. He looked shaken, angry, and ghostly white. Both of my parents mirrored closet doors had been ripped completely from their tracks, and a fine mist of blood sprayed the carpet. Someone was bleeding!

I had no idea whose blood it was—either my dad's or Pop-pop's—but I did learn later that it was Dad who had thrown Pop-pop and Uncle Sammy down the stairs. Physical violence. I was shocked and scared.

That whole scene was frightening. I'd witnessed Dad's temper before, but never could have dreamed he'd get physical with his own dad and brother, let alone throw them bodily down the stairs. I didn't want my young cousins to be party to any possible fallout among Dad, Uncle Sammy, and my grandfather, so I ushered Jonathan, Ilana, and Avi to the other side of the house, well away from the commotion.

The fight had been about my cousins—what else could it have been? Uncle Sammy and Pop-pop had launched a last-ditch attempt to keep Jonathan and Ilana home before they were sent away and separated, which had been met by force from my dad. I think they blamed the boarding school idea on my mom and my dad had become enraged defending her.

Before the plane crash, before my cousins had come to live with us, our lives had been so idyllic. But all that had been upended, even though—to my mind at least—the fighting was all so unnecessary. My parents could easily have absorbed my cousins into their lives, paid for all the help they needed, and carried on as usual. It was my parents' displeasure at being railroaded into caring for three more kids after they'd already raised my sisters and me which had stoked the tension among Dad, Uncle Sammy, and Pop-pop. Furthermore, my parents simply could've allowed the kids to go live with their grandparents.

I once again fell into my role of chief commander and supporter for my dad. Jon and I took my cousins to the airport with my parents. My sisters didn't go. Even as an adult, I felt it was my job to be there for my parents, to be by their side whenever things got rough. It made for an odd dynamic, but it seemed so natural at the time because it was how I'd been raised throughout my entire childhood.

Despite the physical altercation between Dad and Uncle Sammy, Jonathan and Ilana were shipped off to their respective boarding schools, and I prepared to commence my third year of law school.

Chapter Twenty-One:
Haunts Me Today

> *Maybe we all have darkness inside of us and some of us are better at dealing with it than others.*
>
> —Jasmine Warga

Later in my life, when I became a mother, I began to realize how awful it was to send my cousins away. I was sick and questioned everything my parents had always told me. It kept me up at night, it made me cry, it upset me so much I called my sisters. I asked them, "Don't you think it was horrible Mom and Dad sent them to boarding school like that?"

My sisters, even years later, never wanted to discuss any of this with me. I pushed them and asked how they would feel if it was *their* children who had been sent to boarding school just a few years after their parents died. Again, they refused to talk about any of it with me. They repeated that Mom and Dad sent our cousins to the best boarding school and wouldn't hear any argument.

I no longer agree. I was angry and upset with my cousins. At the time, I would *never* go against my parents. I wished I had been stronger then, but I'd been under their spell.

I'm most upset at my part in this: none of us ever visited Jonathan and Ilana while they were away at boarding school. Not Mom, Dad, my sisters, or me. My cousins were out of sight, out of mind, as far as my family were concerned, and I think that must be the most heartbreaking thing of all. If my parents or my sisters ever did visit them, I didn't know about it. It might've been a couple times at most, if any.

It wasn't until twenty-some years later when I finally summoned the courage to confront my mom about the whole sorry episode. My dad had already passed away by then, seven years after the plane crash. I tried to get along with my mom, but we hadn't been the same since my dad died. Confronting her was a big deal for me—and something I was terrified to do.

I told Mom I had been upset, for so many years, about her sending my cousins to boarding school, and asked if maybe she could provide some kind of explanation to make me feel better. She said things weren't working out with Ilana, so my mom had gone to see a psychiatrist. She said the psychiatrist had told her, "Ilana will never be happy in your home," and my cousins would "never be happy living with your 'perfect family.'"

Wait, what?

Yes, that was what Mom told me.

First, I was pretty sure there was no such thing as a *perfect family*, nor that a psychiatrist would make such a statement, especially because she didn't even know the particulars of our family. I couldn't believe what my mom was telling me!

Mom further explained how Ilana went to one of the very best boarding schools on the east coast. That made me even angrier, as it sounded completely ludicrous to me. For birthdays, my cousins were not close enough for us to celebrate with them. I don't remember my parents ever even visiting for Ilana or Jonathan's birthdays. And about when they were sad, lonely, and missing their parents? Who would comfort them? What was wrong with sending them to a school close enough for the family to have dinner with them once a week or to run over if they were having a bad day? Jonathan likely had horrific memories and flashbacks of the crash, and he was only eleven. Who was there for him?

I said all this to my mom, and her trite answer was, "That isn't how boarding schools work." In other words, she was saying you couldn't go pick them up and take them for dinner or have a quick visit as I was suggesting, even if they were close.

What?

Again, *what?*

Those poor kids had lost their parents, and Jonathan was on *the plane*! I was pretty sure schools would make exceptions under such circumstances in the interests of their students' mental wellbeing.

Mom reiterated the "perfect family" issue the psychiatrist described. I eventually found the strength to tell my mom I thought she'd seen a horrible psychiatrist.

Again, I called my sisters and tried to discuss Mom's explanation. And they *again* refused to talk with me. They just didn't want to speak about it, except one of my sisters said our cousins went to an amazing boarding school—the same one Michael Douglas sent his kids.

Who cared?

Nobody in my family sees things the way I do nowadays, and none of them will talk to me about it.

Chapter Twenty-Two:
Ship Them Out Again

We only saw my cousins when they came back to Philly for the holidays. We *all* had to go to the airport to meet them from the plane. Then, the entire family went out to dinner at a favorite fancy restaurant. But far from being a joyous occasion, the whole thing felt decidedly *forced* and uncomfortable.

As time went on, Ilana and Jonathan quite understandably didn't want to go back to Mom and Dad's house. So, my parents drove to New York to meet with Uncle Sammy and Aunt Tris and told them that, since it wasn't working at our house, it was their turn to take my cousins. At least, that was the story my parents told me.

Uncle Sammy had moved back to New York by then, but he said he was perfectly happy taking Ilana and Jonathan. Because he'd accepted, Uncle Sammy received a certain amount of money from his late brother's estate—and, from that day on, my mom and dad explained to me that Sammy had only taken in my cousins for the money!

Uncle Sammy was a successful lawyer who really didn't need the few extra bucks, so I had my doubts as I began to view my parents with different eyes.

And, far from unhappy at being farmed out to New York, both Jonathan and Ilana came to consider Uncle Sammy's house their home. No matter what Uncle Sammy did, though, he couldn't do anything right in my parents' minds. He let Ilana take the subway into the city by herself, something my mom would never allow, and he let Jonathan smoke pot in his room.

"He is a horrible parent!" is all I heard, repeatedly.

Avi had a different relationship with my parents than her siblings. We always described her as Switzerland: Switzerland's foreign policy states that it cannot be involved in armed conflicts between states. Therefore, when people don't want to get involved in other people's issues, they say they want to be Switzerland, and that was what Avi had always been. Today, she attributes her neutrality to the fact she was in a coma for three months and then stayed at McGee rehabilitation where she recovered physically and mentally. She sees it as a gift that she wasn't party to all the fighting and negativity immediately after the crash.

Now, Avi has a great relationship with me, my mom and my sisters. My mom even walked Avi down the aisle at her wedding. Ilana and Jonathan, on the other hand, haven't spoken to my mom for almost thirty years.

Chapter Twenty-Three:
Stress, Engaged

The number one root of all illnesses, as we know, is stress.
—Marianne Williamson

I had just finished finals and was already partying with my friends. My mom called, and I went upstairs where it would be quieter. She told me my dad had had a heart attack, but he was all better now. I didn't know how serious it was because Mom waited until after my finals to tell me, she played it down as "just a warning." Still, I got the impression she wasn't entirely honest with me because she didn't want me worrying about him.

In hindsight, the heart attack was likely due to the huge amount of stress Dad was under, fighting with his family. I can also see now how he was stuck between his family and my mom. The most important thing to him was to make Mom happy and, in that impossible situation, he couldn't. It was, quite literally, worrying him sick!

Dad was a proud family man: he'd taken care of his parents and siblings as well as Mom, my sisters, and me, and that was something that defined him. I can only begin to imagine the impact watching his beloved family falling apart around him must've had on him at the time.

He loved Mom. That was never, ever in question. He also loved his parents and his brother. In action, he wasn't stuck in the middle: he firmly stood by my mother's side and, by defending her, grew further and further apart from his own family. In his heart, he was stuck in the middle.

Unconditional Love

That, I firmly believe, was the root cause of Dad's stress and, ultimately, his heart attacks.

In the middle of all this family chaos, I got engaged! Excited, I wanted my grandparents to meet Jon—I knew they'd love him and be truly happy for me. I arranged for us to go out to dinner. Given the tension between Mom-mom and Pop-pop and my parents, I decided to *just* make it the four of us—but, sadly, my grandparents were *different*. We were different.

We met at Marco Polo. Jon took to them both straightaway. Without knowing how things used to be, he thought their quiet, somewhat guarded demeanor was normal. For me, the whole evening just felt weird: it was like I was eating dinner with a couple of strangers. It was uncomfortable.

After that, I tried my best to regain at least some of the old relationship I'd had with Mom-mom and Pop-pop. After graduating from law school and leaving the bar exam, I wanted to call them like I normally would. So, I did, but it just didn't seem the same. There was so much hostility between them and my parents, and my constant defense of my parents' actions meant going back to the way it used to be became impossible. And yet, through it all, I only ever wanted my mom-mom and Pop-pop back because I missed them.

My mom had never really been close to Mom-mom and Pop-pop in the first place. In fact, other than at family gatherings, she went out of her way to keep her distance. She never spent time with Mom-mom, never sat around the kitchen table, drinking coffee and talking. The only time I remember my mother doing something with Mom-mom was buying her a dress for an affair we were all attending—either a wedding or bar mitzvah. I had the feeling, even as a child, that my mom didn't like my grandparents.

When my parents went away for their annual three-week winter vacation, my grandparents moved into our house and took care of us. Every time they came home, Mom would bluster at how "dirty" the kitchen was. Because I believed everything Mom said, I agreed the kitchen counters were disgusting. Now, as an adult, I would be so glad to go away for three whole weeks, and the least of my worries would be how dirty the kitchen might be upon my return. Especially so if we had a housekeeper who came every day.

I realize now how brainwashed I'd been over my formative years. I'd grown up convinced my grandparents and Uncle Sammy *owed* my parents—and, by default, our family—their lives. Back then, I agreed that my uncle and grandparents had better show up when we needed them.

Did my family even think of the fact that they were also grieving the loss of their brother and their son?

Seems so cold and entitled to me.

Unconditional Love

Through it all, I missed my grandparents terribly. Some years later, they'd moved to Scarsdale to be closer to Uncle Sammy and my cousins. I cried and begged, *pleading* with them to stay, and Dad was so bitterly disappointed he could barely stand to look at them. But they went, nonetheless. In my opinion, it was the final part in the disintegration of the Berger family, and it broke my heart.

What I learned afterwards was that, as soon as my grandparents suggested leaving, my parents immediately put their house up for sale.

Chapter Twenty-Four:
Father's Day

> *Enmeshed families are characterized by levels of emotional closeness that are often seen as constraining. These families use manipulation, usually in the form of overly excessive but superficial expressions of love and unity to demand loyalty from their members.*
>
> —Barbaron & Tirado; Williams & Hiebert

It was 1992, not too long before I got married. I was a full-fledged adult living with Jon, my husband-to-be, in a nice townhouse outside of Philly. I'd managed to land a decent job straight out of law school in the previous December: I was a family law associate in a firm of good standing. I took the bar exam in February 1993 in Pennsylvania and New Jersey and passed both.

A dear friend of mine from high school was getting married. My friends, Andy and Maddie, were living in Michigan and flying into Philly on Saturday for the wedding that night. Since my house was just ten minutes from the venue, Andy and Maddie planned to stay with Jon and I at our townhouse which meant we'd be able to party!

Unfortunately, the timing didn't work out. The wedding fell on the Saturday before Father's Day, which had always been a big event when I was growing up—mostly because Dad enjoyed his daughters worshipping him the entire day. Dad had realized that Father's Day, 1992, was going to be the very last one we would celebrate together before I was married. He wanted me to sleep in my own childhood twin bed one final time and wake up at his house on Father's Day.

Remember, at the time, I lived with Jon.

While the sentiment was sweet and I kind of understood my dad's reasoning, I was a grownup in my twenties and had friends coming over to stay from out of town. Plus, we had made plans to party all night after the wedding.

But Mom was insistent Dad should get what he wanted. Not to mention the full-on guilt trip he gave me about how his little girl was growing up and leaving him and how it was his last chance to enjoy the special day with me. Anyone would have thought the man was dying or I was moving to the other side of the planet, not simply getting married and living just across town from him. In hindsight, I guess it was Dad's way of attempting to recapture the old times and keep hold of his little girl a tad longer.

Not that every Father's Day was a picture of family harmony, by any means. One year, when my sisters and I were very little, Mom bought presents for him on our behalf—as mothers the world over do for kids who are too small to do it themselves. However, when my dad found out what she'd done, and that we hadn't been involved in picking out his gifts at all, he grew furious! It's another one of my earliest memories showcasing his temper.

From that day on, I wrote Dad long letters and chose the most beautiful cards every year. It was a strange dynamic, when I think about it. I inherited his stubborn streak, but in the end, I gave in to his request. It was Mom who *finally* guilted me into acquiescing with her "That's what Dad wants" spiel. Often, she sided with me during Dad's blustering, but on that occasion, she chose to side with him.

And so, I caved to the brainwashing I'd endured throughout my childhood and promised Dad I'd sleep in my old bed so I could wake up to share his special day with him at our family home.

Saturday night, I left my friend's wedding shortly after the post-ceremony banquet, having drunk nothing more than a sip or two of champagne during the toast, and headed straight home to Dad like a dutiful daughter.

On Sunday morning—Father's Day—I wrote my dad a sweet letter.

"Dear Daddy,

I'm so happy that we are all together. You were right, this is such a special morning—all laying together, right when we got up. I really do miss being home and all the special times that go with being with you every day, I guess there does come that time when grow up and now I'm getting married."

At the time, it felt like the most natural thing to do. Sure, I'd been pissed about missing the all-night party with my friends, but my mind had quickly come around to the fact that pandering to my father's whim—even as a supposedly independent adult—had been not only the right thing to do but was a wonderful idea and for the best.

Now, looking back, I see the whole episode as just plain weird—almost disturbing.

Chapter Twenty-Five:
Mr. & Mrs.

Everything moved quickly from our engagement in early '92 to our huge, ridiculously expensive wedding. I'm glad I had the distraction of wedding preparations and studying for the bar exam to take my mind off all the unpleasant feelings swamping my family. I was determined to not allow any of it to mar my big day, and I think the optimist in me hoped my wedding would somehow, magically, bring the estranged family together. I married Jon in April of 1993 at the Ritz Carlton, right in the middle of all the family strife.

The wedding itself was what we'd describe back in the day as "phat" (for the layman, it means something truly excellent and cool). No expense was spared as my parents practically took over the posh Philadelphia Ritz Carlton for their little girl's big, beautiful wedding.

. Mom-mom and Pop-pop came to the wedding, of course. Despite all the tension, I knew they wouldn't have missed it for the world. Even Mom managed to put on a smile for them on the day. After all, what would people have said if my grandparents hadn't been there? What other people thought was always a priority for my parents. Sadly, though, I no longer had the warm, loving relationship I'd once had with Mom-mom and Pop-pop. I'd taken my parents' side in all the drama, and that had pushed them away.

There was more drama before the wedding. But this time it was not with my family. It was with my fiancée's family. To pick the menu for the wedding, Jon and I went to a fancy tasting at the Ritz Carlton about a month before the big day. There, we sampled the luxurious dishes cooked by the hotel's chef, and my parents came along to help with our decision making. (and because they were paying for the wedding).

At one point, the wedding consultant asked Jon about his last name, Waxman, as they were familiar with that name. My future father-in-law and his brothers owned Superior Wine, which supplied wine and liquor and, as it turned out, was a client of the Ritz Carlton. As a result, the hotel offered to allow Mr. Waxman to bring his own wine and alcohol and only charge corkage—to cover the wait staff opening and serving it to the wedding guests.

It seemed an ideal solution: we'd bring in the finest wines and top shelf alcohol through my future husband's family business for our wedding, and it would save my father a small fortune in purchasing drinks at retail cost from the hotel. Considering Dad was forking out a lot of money for the wedding, it would have been a nice gesture on the Waxman's' part.

However, Jon's father flatly refused. Jon asked his cousin, who also worked at the company, to help us bring the alcohol in for the wedding. Jon couldn't get anyone in his family to agree.

Dad went crazy! "That man's a loser!" he snapped as we left the tasting room. "He's paid for *nothing* so far. I'm going to go see him." Despite my mom's protests, Dad set off to find Jon's father. I never knew about this until years later.

Dad went to the Waxman's' home, where he shoved Jon's dad up against the wall and explained as calmly as he could that he *really* ought to be supplying the wine and alcohol for the ceremony.

Shaken, scared witless by my father, Mr. Waxman still refused to play along and didn't provide one drop for our wedding, nor did he offer to pay for anything my dad bought. In the end, because the Ritz Carlton purchased from Superior Wines, my father-in-law made a tidy profit from his own son's wedding!

Jacob and Martine flew to Philadelphia for my wedding. While at my parent's house, Jacob picked the Jewish Exponent, a small newspaper, up from the coffee table and began looking through it. He stopped on a certain page, took the paper to show my Dad, and pointed to a watch and store and asked my dad to take him. Dad obliged, and they headed to Govbergs, a posh jewelry store. When they arrived, Jacob explained to my dad that he saw me admiring Martine's Cartier watch and he wanted to buy me one as a wedding gift. He picked out a beautiful diamond-encrusted watch for $14,600—money really was no object for our Parisian friends—but my father told him no, they couldn't buy it for me. In Dad's mind, it was far too extravagant, even though it was an everyday watch compared to some of Cartier's other products.

But Jacob insisted. He and my dad argued in the store. Jacob said it was *his* decision to make, not Dad's, and went right ahead and paid for that posh watch despite the protestations. Unfortunately, though, my father's disapproval resulted in a physical altercation right there in the jewelry store! They would laugh about it afterward, and they reminisced about the story with me every time I went to Govbergs to have my watch repaired.

Nevertheless, Jacob bought the Cartier and presented it to me.

Now, here comes the crazy part.

Remember, I was a grown woman, old enough to get married, yet my parents *forbade* me from wearing that watch! Eventually, after I begged, they gave in but on one condition. They wanted to hold on to the watch, my own wedding gift, "for safe keeping," and I had to ask Mom for it when I wanted to wear it. So, whenever I attended a wedding or a fancy affair, I had to ask my mother if I could wear *my* watch—and I'd have to go over to her house and get it from her.

Then—and here's the really fucked up part—I dutifully handed it back to her when I was finished with it! Without question.

I'd been raised to never question my parents' demands, no matter how odd and controlling they seemed at the time. Not *once* did I even contemplate keeping my watch or refusing to give it back, even though I was a grown-ass, married woman.

Finally, many years later, my parents gave it back.

Thanks!

***

Putting all of that—as well as my own family's issues—aside, I was determined to thoroughly enjoy my two-week honeymoon in Hawaii. I'd earned it, after all!

A couple days into our vacation, a strange thing happened. It had been a long while since I'd witnessed the kind of antisemitic prejudice I'd been warned about as a kid, and I'd naïvely thought it was all behind me as an adult.

Jon was a keen golfer and determined to make the most of the Mauna Lani resort's world-famous golf course. I'm not as enthusiastic—my interest in the sport went about as far as the tiny putt-putt courses with the little windmills—so I was happy to ride around in the cart from hole to hole while Jon played.

On our first day on the course, we were paired with another newlywed couple from the resort—the organizers must've figured we'd have plenty to talk about. The couple, Chuck and Cindy, were from Dallas, Texas, and we hit it off straightaway. Recently, the Dallas Cowboys had been in the playoffs against the Eagles, and commercials played in Philly for the best food in Dallas and vice versa. Jon had appeared in one of the Dallas commercials for Hoagies. Chuck said he thought Jon looked familiar, and we eventually figured out why. Crazy!

Unconditional Love

Cindy and I took turns driving the golf cart and chatting as we followed our husbands around the greens. She suggested when we reached the ninth hole—the halfway point—we'd supported our husbands enough and planned to head to the pool for a dip, lunch, and cocktails.

How could I possibly have said no?

As we drove, talk inevitably turned to weddings. Cindy told me all about her big day, and I described some of the customs associated with a Jewish wedding, such as Bede ken, in which the groom veils his wife's face to signify that his love is for her inner beauty and that he understands they both remain individuals after the marriage. I reminisced about getting married under a chuppah and breaking the glass.

When we arrived at the next hole, I climbed out, but Cindy stayed in the cart. And then again at the next hole. I noticed she'd grown quiet, which I assumed was due to boredom watching the guys play golf. Or maybe I'd talked a little too much?

At the ninth hole, she finally climbed out of the cart, and I assumed we'd head off to the pool as she'd suggested.

But no.

Without a word, Cindy wandered off across the green and headed back in the direction of the hotel. She never once looked back or offered any kind of explanation.

Chuck, who appeared mortified by his new wife's behavior, said quietly, face red with embarrassment, "Cindy has never been exposed to Jews before, and she just doesn't like them." The poor guy couldn't apologize enough, and the atmosphere was more than awkward as he and Jon finished up their game and I trundled behind them in the little cart. I still wonder if their marriage lasted much beyond the honeymoon or if a bigoted attitude toward Jewish people was the norm back in Texas. Maybe Chuck and Cindy considered they'd had a narrow escape from socializing with Jon and me.

It was a firsthand experience with antisemitism in 1993! We grow up knowing people don't like us because we're Jewish. We are also instructed to be proud of who we are and to ignore what others think of us.

Chapter Twenty-Six:
The Honeymoon's Over

When Jon and I returned to our everyday lives, I received notification that I'd passed the Pennsylvania and New Jersey bar exam I'd taken in February—it was cause for a double celebration! I was working hard as a family law attorney, but I really wanted to get pregnant and become a mom.

I've come to realize how the way my parents treated me was not only about what was best for me but just as much about controlling me. Their influence extended far beyond my childhood days, continuing into my adult life with an iron grip.

When I married and moved out of the family home, my parents' influence expanded to include my husband. When we were down the shore with my parents, he and I were not allowed to go out to dinner with friends because we had to have dinner with the family, every night, namely Dad.

Yes, I did say *allowed*!

We went to a different restaurant every night, fancy, expensive restaurants… and I didn't know anything different. We could meet our friends at the bars after dinner. And that's what we did.

Also, while vacationing at the condo, the golden rule was no one could go to the beach until everyone got up and ate breakfast together. We had to sit around and wait, no matter how hungry we were or how eager to enjoy the sunshine outside—and that was the way things were, even after I was married! I never thought anything of it. It was just our routine. When my husband wanted to go to

Unconditional Love

the beach around nine one morning when everyone else was still sleeping, I told him he couldn't. I said, "When you have your own condo down the shore, you can go to the beach whenever you want, but while we're staying with my parents, we must do what they want." And I was happy to enforce the rules. Didn't see anything weird about it.

Just as bizarre as how I was never allowed to leave my parents' side to sit on the beach with my friends. All the teenagers sat together on the beach, down near Lucy the Elephant, and I was never allowed. I was permitted to walk down and say hi, but that was it. This controlling behavior invaded my marriage. One Saturday, our friends Annina and Kevin drove down the shore to spend the day with my husband and me. They didn't want to sit on the beach with my parents, they wanted to smoke some pot, drink a little, and listen to the Grateful Dead at high volume. But I was not allowed to take my chair or Jon's chair to sit with our friends. We had to stay with my family. So, Jon and I remained with my parents, while Annina and Kevin sat fifty feet behind us. If you can imagine, this was ridiculous, and I was married! I'm still friends with Annina, and occasionally we talk about how fucked up that was.

It's difficult to pinpoint exactly when I had the epiphany because it kind of crept up on me, but I think I began to see my family life as less than normal the more I became exposed to the outside world. I am not a child anymore, I am a grown adult, married, and I know that I still must sit with my family on the beach. No matter what.

Looking back, I can see now just how unhealthy being part of that enmeshed family really was.

This control also spread into my legal career.

As was normal for me, my parents had gotten me the job. They knew a judge who was of counsel with the firm as well as my boss, the senior partner. My boss was mean and misogynistic, overlooking all the good work I did. I might have hated the job, but I'd been raised to always bring my A game—and I was damned good at it! Nevertheless, I was ignored every time I dared speak up! It was a crappy environment for any woman, me especially.

One time, my friend Marlyn's bachelorette party was on a Friday night, and my boss asked me to be at work on Saturday morning at 7 a.m. to help him prepare for trial. I explained how I had a prior engagement that would keep me out late Friday night and asked if there was any way I could come in a little later, like 9am. He said absolutely not.

I went to the bachelorette party and had a great time. I set my alarm early and made it to work by 7 a.m., a little hungover and hungry. However, my boss *never* showed up! Not at all. We didn't have cell phones back then, and I tried to call him at home—but he just didn't answer. That's just one example of how I was treated.

Another time, there was a bad snowstorm. I was on the PA turnpike and driving conditions were worsening. I pulled over to call work and ask my boss if I should still come in or if I could work from home. He told me I still needed to come in. So, I drove through dangerous icy conditions to get to work. Guess what? He'd already left to go home, and the office was closed.

The worst was when I was assigned to prepare a brief and memorandum for a Superior Court Appeal. In a Superior Court Appeal, you ask the Superior Court to determine that the Lower Court has made a mistake, and their ruling should be overturned. This is not easy. I was given no guidance or any direction on what issues to address. After completion, my boss stood in front of my desk and read through the brief. When he finished, he dropped it on my desk and told me it was horrible. Horrible? It had to be filed tomorrow.

They submitted and filed my brief, exactly the way I wrote it. Guess what? We won the appeal, and the Lower Court's ruling was overturned. My boss walked up and down the halls of the law firm, expressing his pride and excitement. He walked right by my office and never said a word to me. Nothing. He then invited the client to his office for a champagne celebration. He also invited his paralegal. I was excluded. He never acknowledged my work or the success I achieved for him. As you can imagine, I hated my job so much!

But… my parents wouldn't *allow* me to quit.

Yes, I was twenty-five, married, and a lawyer, and my mom and dad wouldn't let me leave a job in which I was miserable. Because I'd been indoctrinated to never quit and to *always* mind my parents, I stuck with that job for the remainder of the year and bid my time.

Since they were creatures of habit, I knew my parents would leave for their annual winter vacation. That year, they would travel to Thailand. Knowing they'd not be back for three weeks; I planned to hand in my notice the moment my parents were out of the country and escape that horrible firm before they got back! They couldn't do a thing about it other than express their displeasure at my subversive, defiant actions.

So, I gave my G-d-awful boss my notice—he seemed surprised—worked my two weeks and got out of there while Mom and Dad were out of the country. By the time they returned home, I'd landed myself a part-time position at a small family law firm working for a nice guy named Mark. Even though it was still family law, I was much more appreciated there, Mark listened to me and took on board some of my suggestions. He also praised my hard work, which certainly made for a refreshing change.

As predicted, my parents were bitterly disappointed in my decision, although it was tempered a little by the fact that I wasn't sitting at home unemployed. Plus, there was nothing they could do to stop me, even if they considered it a reckless and foolish decision.

As it worked out in the end, I wasn't with Mark all that long before I started to get morning sickness. I practiced law until I became pregnant with my first baby—Josh—in April 1995, at which time I quit to be a full-time mom.

Chapter Twenty-Seven:
Violent Endings

It's sad how family members can tear each other apart with their words and actions, when they should be a pillar of support and love.

—Unknown

The hatred between my uncle and aunt and my parents came to a head in 1995. By that time, it was an all-out war between Mom and Dad, my grandparents, Uncle Sammy and Aunt Tris. Or to be more accurate, it was me and my parents against the rest—because I always took what Mom and Dad told me as complete gospel and sprang to their defense no matter what.

I vividly recall the next violent Berger encounter, when I was pregnant with Josh, and we went to Uncle Sammy and Aunt Tris's for the Jewish holiday Passover. It was terrifying. My parents rented a van, and we all packed in - my family, my husband and my sister's boyfriend. We knew it would be uncomfortable, but we drove over two hours to try make things right in our family. The tension between Mom and Dad and Sammy and Tris was palpable from the moment they were all in the same room together. Despite the hostility felt by all sitting around the dining room table, we performed the Passover Seder. The Passover Seder is a festive meal and ritual that celebrates the story of the Jewish people's freedom from slavery in Egypt. Together we read from the Haggadah, which explains the foods, recounts the story of the Exodus, and provides instructions for the order of the meal. Side by side we said prayers, sang songs and ate all the food one is required to eat from the Seder Plate. This was followed by a typical Passover dinner consisting of matzah ball soup, gefilte fish, brisket, potato kugel and lots of matzah with butter and salt.

Unfortunately, it turned into the worst night of all.

As we were getting ready to leave, Dad popped his head into the kitchen where Aunt Tris was washing the dishes and rudely and *very* sarcastically said, "Thanks a lot, Tris."

In the blink of an eye, Dad and Uncle Sammy's voices raised and tempers flared once again.

Uncle Sammy grabbed my dad, and I, despite being pregnant, tried to pull my them apart. In the process, Sammy's glasses were knocked off his face. We were in a three-way brawl in the middle of the kitchen!

Uncle Sammy yelled to get out of his house as the fight moved toward the front door into the foyer. Unexpectedly, Jon jumped on Uncle Sammy and put him in a headlock. I was pregnant, so I understood his caveman instinct kicking in to protect me.

Jon would not release my uncle, and my mom had to separate them. By that point, we were outside the house, brawling on the front lawn like a bunch of hooligans, but still the fighting didn't stop. In fact, it escalated.

Uncle Sammy's neighbors, who also attended the Passover dinner, sat on the front steps of the house watching the entire scene with shocked amusement on their faces. My cousin Jonathan scrambled away down the dark street. My sister and Aunt Tris yelled at each other; their faces almost touching. I had no doubt somebody would call the police soon!

Uncle Sammy called my mom a bitch and I was stunned. *Nobody* said that about my mom!

All of our behavior was frightful, disgraceful and beyond appalling. A second round of physical violence. It was devastating.

Eventually, thankfully, things calmed down enough for us to climb into the big van we had rented to drive to NY and retreat to our hotel. Because I was pregnant, I couldn't drink or partake in anything to calm my nerves. Meanwhile, my sisters, their boyfriend, and my husband smoked weed and got drunk. Everybody was in shock!

I can honestly say it was the most unspeakable terrible experience I have ever had in my entire life. It illustrated to me that the tensions within my family had boiled over into something altogether more disturbing. It had morphed into something physical and violent. And it didn't help that my cousins were seeing it all happen, again!

What was happening to my family?

Chapter Twenty-Eight:
New Beginnings- My Josh

My son was born on December 6, 1995. I went into the hospital at 7 a.m. and didn't have Josh until twenty hours later. Not only did I have to push for the last three hours but the doctor ultimately had to use forceps to get him out! Both families waited in the visitor's lounge. They made a list of everyone's guesses for Josh's estimated time of arrival. Whoever was closest got to be the first one to greet my new beautiful baby boy. The doctors had to stitch me up, and I didn't get to hold my baby until forty minutes after he was born. As with Jewish tradition, we are not allowed to name our children after those that are living. Instead, we name our children after those passed to honor their memory. (I think this is just Ashkenazi Jews, which I am. I think Sephardic Jews do name after those living. But that's too deep of a discussion for this book. Ha!) We use either the full name or an initial. Josh is named after my mom's father, Joseph and his middle name, Matthew, is named after my husband's grandmother, Margaret.

I don't remember filling out the hospital menu for breakfast the next morning, but I somehow wrote in "chocolate ice cream," which they did bring me. Ha! My husband slept in the room on a small cot and when we woke up, he complained about how much his back hurt and how terribly he slept. Meanwhile, I'd just had a baby, and my crotch felt like it was so swollen I could hardly move. And his back hurt?

As Jewish tradition dictated, we held his bris when Josh was eight days old. The bris is the first time a child is celebrated in Jewish culture. We don't subscribe to the American tradition of baby showers—no gifts are given until *after* the child is born. In fact, nothing is permitted to be bought before birth at all, including furniture, clothes, and the myriad paraphernalia necessary to take care of a newborn. Everything is ordered ahead, though, and scheduled for delivery after the birth. The nursery room stands empty and bare; the only thing we're allowed to do is paint it.

It's traditional among the more affluent Jews in my area to have a nurse attend the newborn, staying at the home for the two weeks following the birth. I was grateful—taking care of a baby is exhausting—and my parents were only too delighted to hire one. While I was in the hospital, they arranged for all the baby furniture to be delivered and our nurse, Darlene, would set about putting Josh's room together.

Darlene had a huge personality, sported maroon cornrows, and stood at six-foot-three. She pulled up in a brand-new Infinity and moved in with us for the entire two weeks after I left the hospital and handled everything. She did all the cooking, cleaning, and taking care of the baby so I could get some rest and recoup my energy. She taught me everything I needed to know about being a mom and how to care for my son. Most importantly, she allowed me to get the rest I needed and was an invaluable source of information, especially about how to set schedules and routines. I had never babysat as a teen and didn't really know much about babies.

The bris, or Brit Milah as it's more commonly known, is a sacred Jewish ceremony in which baby boys are circumcised. It's *expected* in our culture, going all the way back to the Book of Genesis: G-d commanded Abraham to circumcise himself and his male children as a sign of the covenant between the Jewish people and Himself.

The bris is an important occasion, attended by only immediate family and closest friends. It's held at home and performed on a table, rather than at the hospital in an operating room. The actual circumcision is performed by the mohel, who is paid to come to the house. The mohel is typically a physician, rabbi, cantor, midwife, or nurse. Every mohel is fully trained in Jewish laws regarding circumcision and modern surgical hygiene.

Having never been party to a bris, I was nervous. But having my family around made me proud. It was nice to have my family together; even though the tension was still there, they were all on their very best behavior.

Tradition dictates that the baby's godmothers, my sister and Jon's sister, carry him into the kitchen and hand him over to the sandek—the person who will hold him during the procedure. The role of the sandek is typically performed by a grandparent. We chose my dad, who refused to even look while the actual circumcision was performed. Pictures show my dad holding Josh down by his little ankles with my dad's head at a 90-degree angle facing the opposite direction.

After reciting the blessings, the mohel got to work. To placate the baby, a Q-tip dipped in wine is given to the infant to suck on while the procedure is performed. It's a day of mixed emotions for a new, young mother who'd never experienced a bris before there's the pride of introducing her newborn son to the family and the Jewish faith, the feeling of love surrounded by family and friends, all mixed with concern about her child's wellbeing. I had nothing to worry about, of course, because Josh was well taken care of.

In addition to the bris, if the firstborn child is a boy and he is considered not to be in the priestly class but is an Israelite, we perform a special ceremony thirty days after his birth. The Pidyon Haben (which literally means "redemption of the firstborn son") stems from the ancient belief that Israelite Jews are the lowest "caste," and are therefore to be looked down upon. The male baby's father must buy five special, expensive coins from Israel to give to the Kohen (the Hebrew word for priest) *to* purchase redemption for his son.

My parents' attorney and friend purchased those coins directly from Israel and gave them to us for Josh's baby gift. I had never seen such coins before, and they were very, very special to me. I kept them after the ceremony and held onto them until after my divorce many years later, at which point I sold them. I had to pay my bills somehow.

I remember well, when my dad was planning one of Mom's birthday parties, he called the leader of the band we normally used at our parties, Eddie Bruce, and asked about some venues other than the usual fancy hotels, - The Four Seasons, The Rittenhouse Hotel, The Ritz Carlton. Eddie Bruce, who would perform at my wedding and my son's bar mitzvah, was the frontman to one of the best, most popular party bands in the Philadelphia area and from the all the parties my parents had with him as the band leader, he developed a special friendship with my parents. He took my dad out for the day. One of the venues he showed him was the Pyramid Club, which was where my mom's birthday party was. The Pyramid Club was the first private club in Philadelphia. This exclusive club is on the 52nd floor, up in the sky, with floor to ceiling windows displaying the most beautiful views of the city of Philadelphia.

My dad developed a special connection with Tim, the manager of the Pyramid Club, and had my mom's surprise fortieth birthday party there. Their relationship got us into all the highly prestigious parties—Valentines and Mother's Day, to name two. Tim even got me and my husband four seats to the New Year's Eve party, and we went with my friends Andy and Maddie. We were all dressed up, black tie, and rented a limousine for the night. That one was so wild revelers were openly doing lines of cocaine off the bathroom floor!

The Pyramid Club was where my parents hosted Josh's Pidyon Haben! It was like a wedding or bar mitzvah, and it was fabulous! For the *Pidyon Haben*, my parents booked the exceptionally talented, golden-voiced Eddie Bruce and his orchestra to provide the entertainment!

My son's *Pidyon Haben* was a wonderful time, even amid all the family strife. I look back upon it with fondness but also with a heavy heart because it highlighted how magical my family's relationships had once been, before the plane crash. It also marked the last happy occasion before Dad's untimely death, just two and a half years later, when I was pregnant with his second grandchild and the one, I'd name in his honor, Bari Leigh.

Chapter Twenty-Nine:
Unhappy Families

Grief is like the ocean, it comes in waves, ebbing and flowing. Sometimes the water is calm, and sometimes it is overwhelming. All we can do is learn to swim.

—Vicki Harrison

"It's not healthy," Jon moaned. It wasn't the first time he'd brought up the closeness between me and my family, and I knew damn well it wouldn't be the last.

"Dad just wants to be with us," I replied.

"We've spent more of our married life over at their house than we have here!" My husband's exaggeration wasn't too far from the truth; having grown up so close to my family, it just seemed natural to spend as much time with them as possible. I couldn't see the strong influence Mom and Dad exerted over me—even as a grown-up, married mother.

"You know that's not true." My protest fell on deaf ears. "They love seeing Josh, and he loves spending time with his grandparents."

"Yeah, but that's *all* they do. They don't have any friends other than us and your sisters."

"Mom and Dad have loads of friends!" I argued with a sigh.

My parents *did* have friends, ones who went all the way back to their college days. When I was growing up, my parents went out every Saturday night with another couple or couples. But that was it. Other than those nights, I rarely saw my mom meet friends for lunch or shopping, and I *never* saw my dad go out with just the guys. We had season tickets for the Flyers and Eagles games, and my dad's first choice was *always* us girls. If we couldn't go to a game with him, then—*and only then*—my dad would ask his friends. That was the only time my dad hung out with his pals without Mom. When I was young, Dad took my mom to the Flyers games just for her to sit there and read a book she'd brought; sports bored her to tears, unless it was the playoffs, which she enjoyed. My dad only wanted to be with his wife and daughters. Friends came second.

"It's just not... *healthy*, Stacey." Jon always said when we had this discussion. I'd argue black was white when it came to my parents. At that point in my life, I believed we had the best family, and we were lucky to be so close.

I would later learn my family relationships were *not* so healthy.

When my son Josh was born, I asked my mom to babysit for me so I could attend a girls' luncheon. This luncheon was happening in a month and on a weekday. My mom said she could babysit for me, *but* she wouldn't be able to help if it was raining because my dad was a landscaper, and he didn't work when it rained. My mom couldn't even leave him for those couple hours, and she didn't offer to watch Josh at her house. When Dad was home, she had to stay there with him.

Since bonds were so strained between my parents and my grandparents and uncle, and Mom and Dad never had much to do with Mom's side of the family, Jon and I were "it" for them. Still, for the next couple of years or so, up to 1998, I maintained the status quo despite my husband's protestations, and we continued to spend most of our free time with my parents.

Although I was focused upon my marriage to Jon and our son, my husband couldn't compete with the overwhelming love and support I'd always received from my parents. They'd always been there for me and continued to be so throughout those early years of my marriage.

It's important to remember that, up until then, I was always the "fixer" for my family: whenever something happened, be it something trivial or the devastating loss of my aunt and uncle in the plane crash, good ol' Stacey was always there to fetch and carry, to play taxi night and day, and to comfort those who needed it most, even if it was at the expense of my husband and son. My sisters rarely stepped up to help—even in the aftermath of the crash, the best they could do was sit in Mom and Dad's house and mourn while I ferried visitors to and from the airport, back and forth to their hotels and made sure everyone had plenty to eat and drink.

But no matter how one-sided the whole thing was, I carried on regardless. It was just what I did, and I never got mad at my sisters. It was just a fact: if my parents needed help, I jumped.

Unconditional Love

After my cousins were so unceremoniously shipped off to separate boarding schools and my parents' monumental falling out with my grandparents, Uncle Sammy and Aunt Tris, I saw a less-than-subtle change in my father. On the outside, he appeared to be the same outgoing, generous family man everyone knew and loved, but on the inside, in private and when he thought no one was looking, he was altogether different: a withdrawn shell of the wonderful man he once was.

My poor father was broken.

He so desperately wanted to be close to his parents. He asked me many times to talk to my mom and see if she could accept them despite their differences. Of course, I could never bring that up with my mother. I was far too scared to confront her, and certainly so if she was with either of my sisters. To the three of them, it was all about appearances and maintaining the façade of normality, even though my family was essentially at war with itself and had just been through a tragedy that might tear any other family completely apart.

On top of that, my parents always told us to never talk to our friends about what was happening at home. I followed that rule until I got older and realized how messed up my family really was.

I tried talking to Jon. He repeated that my family just wasn't normal. He loved all the vacations, shows, sporting events, and expensive restaurants my parents treated us to, but eventually he realized we only ever spent time with my family. And I was content with that. I was so proud of my family and loved being around them. When I wasn't allowed to hang out with friends on a Saturday night because we had to go out with Mom and Dad, I didn't know any difference. I simply embraced our quirks.

However, even though I was married, a mother, and an attorney, my parents still directed my life and made decisions for me. And I knew my dear father was hurting inside—badly. The falling out, especially the physical fights with his dad and brother, had wounded him to his very core.

Dad had spent a lot of time, trouble, and money to take care of my grandparents. He saw their lack of support following the crash as not only ungrateful, but the ultimate betrayal. My mother's poisonous words about parents' disloyalty chipped away at him, to the point Dad forgot that they, too, had suffered an insurmountable loss when that plane went down. Dad had lost his brother, but my grandparents lost their son. I can't even begin to imagine how terrible that must have been for them.

My dad told me how he would go to my grandparents' house and drop off donuts for them on the hood of their car in the driveway before sneaking away. I imagined him driving slowly, carefully, through the early morning Philadelphia streets. As with any other large city, the roads contained enough cars, vans, and trucks to make one wonder just what the heck all those people had to do—or where they were possibly going—at such an ungodly hour. He arrived in a part of the city only a few blocks from my grandparents' house. He slowed in front of a small strip mall and pulled into the largely empty parking lot. Still early, all the little shop fronts were dark, except one…

Meyer's Family Donut. The lights were on, the red neon sign above the door declared the place to be open for business, and there was a small line of early risers waiting patiently inside to be served. The aroma of fresh-cooked donuts and bagels wafted through the air. They were Pop-pop's favorite donuts in the entire city.

I envisioned Dad through the store window as he chatted with others in the line and engaged in light-hearted banter with the proprietor. She was the young lady who'd taken over in recent years from her parents, the original Meyers. It was pleasant to see Dad smile and laugh.

With a bulging bag of donuts clutched in one hand, my father probably left a substantial tip into the wide-necked jar on the countertop and made his way out of the store. The tiny bell above the door tinkled as it opened, and more of that delicious smell escaped out into the dark morning.

My heart thumped high in my throat as I imagined Dad's car along the familiar route to my grandparents' house—the one he'd bought and paid for so they could live out their twilight years in comfort, free from financial worries. Of course, he got himself a donut too and was eating his Boston cream donut, making a mess, while he drove. Donuts were freshest in the early hours, and the furtiveness to not tell my mom was to avoid her inevitable cross-examinations and judgement. As far as she was concerned, the Bergers were at war, and there was to be no fraternizing with the enemy who had so blatantly let her and my father down.

When my dad told me how he quietly walked up to my pop-pop's car, dropped the bag of donuts off on the hood, and hurried back to his own, my heart broke into a thousand pieces.

I recall a conversation with Dad not too long afterward. We were having brunch at the Yorktown Inn—they had the best eggs benedict and peach pie—and he asked me again if… *how*… I could possibly get my mother to understand that my grandparents were simply different from her and if she could ever understand and accept that. We compared a Sprite and a Coke as an example; one could never be the other, but you can still like both.

There was no doubt in my mind they *had* done what they thought was expected of them, if not more so, in the aftermath of the crash by taking care of their grandchildren. Anything lacking was merely in my parents' mind. But inside,

I really felt like my mom's expectations hadn't been met, and she had taken that as a slight against her and my father.

I wanted to tell Mom about Dad's secret donut gifts, but I knew that would break his confidence and could result in even more discord between my parents. They had been through more than enough already. And quite frankly, I was afraid to tell my mom.

So, it festered, like some open sore weighing, on my father's shoulders—one more piece of pain to hide behind his brave face. I honestly believe the emotional wounds killed him.

The winter of '97 and '98, Mom and Dad jetted off for their annual vacation, this time to New Zealand and Australia. Jon, Josh—who was only two years old—and I waved them off at the airport. It was all smiles, business as usual.

My dad was so paranoid about his health that right before their trip to Australia and New Zealand, he took a stress test for his heart. Back in those days, they didn't have the Thallium Stress Test, in which they inject dye into the heart to find out if any of the arteries were closed off. The regular stress tests my dad had undergone only shows if more than one artery is blocked. It failed to show the one clogged artery he was apparently suffering from. The only thing the cardiologists could do was open him up and look for themselves at what was going on.

My parents had barely gotten to their exotic destination when I discovered some important news to send them. I faxed it to their hotel the moment I found out.

Hi. Guess what? We are pregnant!

I'd only just found out I was expecting their second grandchild.

My parents returned from their vacation around the middle of January 1998 and, two months later, the Berger family was beset by yet another heartbreaking tragedy.

Chapter Thirty:
End of an Era

The loss you feel when a loved one dies is not the worst feeling in the world. Missing them for the rest of your life is worse.

—Unknown

When Mom and Dad returned from their winter vacation to New Zealand and Australia, Dad and I went to the Flyers game. That was one of my favorite things to do with my dad and something we'd done since I was a little girl. The Flyers usually played Tuesday, Thursday, and Sunday. We had two season tickets at the Spectrum, Section L-M, row 19. My sisters and I took turns going to the games with Dad; we called it a "date" because we also got to go to South Philly for a nice dinner beforehand. This was a Berger family tradition, which Dad kept up for as long as I can remember.

That year, 1998, it was my turn to go on the Flyers "date," which sadly turned out to be the last game I would ever attend with Dad. It was a coincidence I would treasure for the rest of my life.

As always, Dad made the outing a special occasion. He made *every* one of our outings special; he was never one for half-measures. "Go big or go home" for him was more than a motto—it was a lifelong *philosophy*!

Our adventure began with dinner at one of Dad's favorite Italian restaurants in South Philadelphia. That's where all the good Italian restaurants were, according to him, and he was well-known in most, if not all, of them. Dad maintained that the very best food in Philly wasn't at the big, fancy restaurants and *not* in any of the chain establishments, but in the small, family-owned places. He sought out the smallest, coziest Mom and Pop Italian restaurants—those which more resembled someone's front room than an eatery—and took us there for our pre-game dinner. The owners of whichever restaurant Dad decided upon knew him and welcomed us with open arms and the broadest of smiles. I felt like royalty walking into those places. It was a sensation I'd gotten used to around my father—everybody who ever met him absolutely *loved* him, not just because he supported small businesses and tipped so generously. I could tell from a very young age people *genuinely* loved Dad and enjoyed his patronage and company.

After eating, it was time to head down to the game. We had the same parking arrangement we had at the Eagles games. Jerry was the head of parking, and my dad beeped to let him know we were there. Jerry opened the chained fence, and Dad backed into a spot that only had room for two cars.

Despite how full we were, Dad and I always got peanut chews or ice cream at the game, and sometimes Dad bought me a new Flyers sweatshirt. The same people sat in our section at the Spectrum for years and became our friends. I forget the name of the big guy who used to sit behind us, but on the last two seats of the aisle were Al and his son. When I went to a game while pregnant with Josh, Al gifted me infant Flyers socks.

A couple days after that Flyers game, I received a phone call from my mother.

I was relaxing at home on Sunday evening, newly pregnant with my daughter, sitting on the couch watching a James Woods movie. My husband was at work. Josh scampered around, playing with his Legos and getting ready to go to sleep.

The phone, one of those old-style rotary things, sat on a small table next to the couch. It was strategically placed so neither Jon nor I would have to get up to answer it. It was getting late in the evening—we *never* received calls so late—and its harsh trill startled me.

"Stacey?" Something in the voice immediately struck me as odd. It was almost as if my mother was surprised, I'd answered my own telephone.

"Oh, hi, Mom."

"It's your dad." Mom's voice trembled a little, which heightened my concern. She rarely showed any level of emotion like that.

"Is he okay?" I knew it was a dumb question even as I asked it—Mom wouldn't disturb me in the evening if everything was okay. But it was all I could think of to ask.

"Something's wrong, Stacey," Mom told me. "With your father. He just said he felt a little unwell, but I could see he was trying to downplay it. You know how he is."

Unconditional Love

I understood all too well. Dad did everything he could possibly do to not have people worry about him. That he'd even said *something* about not feeling too well to Mom spoke volumes.

"He's in the ambulance." Her voice cracked, and my blood ran cold. "They're taking him to the hospital right now. Meet us there, I love you." she said before hanging up without a goodbye.

I immediately called my husband and told him something happened to my dad, that he was in an ambulance on his way to the hospital. Josh looked at me, curious from the tone in my voice and no doubt alarmed by the grim look on my face—I felt the color draining from it even as I spoke.

"I have to get there," I told Jon, my feelings numb. "Now. You need to come home and stay with Josh."

Even though I lived fifteen minutes from the hospital, the drive felt like one of the longest of my life. I'd jumped straight into the car the moment Jon pulled into the driveway. I was acting on autopilot, my mind spinning elsewhere as I went through the motions of getting to Mom and Dad as quickly as possible. *Why would Dad take an ambulance to the hospital and not have Mom drive him?*

My dad had never been sick before—*really* sick, I mean. Sure, he'd suffered that minor heart attack way back when I was taking my finals in law school, but it had been of so little concern to him that he'd chosen not to tell me and risk harming my exam results. Which brought my mind back to the question, *why is he in an ambulance?*

It's not like Dad lived in constant denial, though. I know so many people who assume they're immortal because they don't need to visit the doctor. Not my dad. He constantly feared getting sick—maybe because both his parents had heart disease and high cholesterol. He tried to stay fit and eat well. Mom packed him healthy lunches and cooked deliciously nutritious dinners. He walked on the treadmill (in his jockey underwear) and ate frozen yogurt with pretzels for a snack when he would much rather have had a hot fudge sundae. I believe his desire to be in good shape was all part of his role as the Great Provider for his beloved family: if he got sick, his position would be compromised. He'd even gotten a stress test before flying out to New Zealand that winter—all results came back clear—and he worked out regularly, ate sensibly, and didn't drink or smoke. My memories of Dad were of a fit, healthy guy who *I* thought would live forever.

Arriving at the hospital in record time, I found Mom in the waiting area, her expression gray, slack, filled with worry. She always dressed sharp with a full face of make-up, but that night, she wore sweat socks with her slippers and was completely disheveled.

"Your father had a seizure, Stacey," she told me, her voice barely a whisper.

"A *seizure*?" I tried and failed not to sound incredulous. "Dad's *never* been epileptic!"

Mom half-shrugged her shoulders. "Well, he had a seizure. The paramedics told me that's what it was when they got to the house. That's why I called 911."

I figured she'd panicked and knew she had no chance of getting Dad to the car if he was unresponsive. I felt bad that she was clearly beating herself up about the whole episode. "You did the right thing, Mom," I soothed her the best I could. I was sure she could see the turmoil I was going through. "He's in the best place now. They'll get him fixed right up."

I found out later my father had been feeling unwell since the Thursday before, *three days* before his seizure. He'd complained to Mom about a pain in his jaw and another pain which ran down his arm. Even though they were classic heart attack symptoms, on Friday he went off to work as usual. He reassured my mother he felt much, much better and she didn't need to worry about him.

But he returned home at 2:00 in the afternoon, which was something he never did. *Never*. Dad was always the last one to leave a job site and, often, worked late. Even on Fridays.

Mom told me later he was running a high fever when he got home. She had no idea that was also a symptom of a heart attack, and she brushed it off as a touch of the "Flu, at the very worst."

Healthcare was nowhere near as fiercely regulated back in the 1990s as it is now, and pharmacists regularly dished out antibiotics without a prescription, especially if they knew the patient well. My mother had taken it upon herself to put Dad on antibiotics. She did this a lot whenever my sisters or me got sick, our whole lives. Expecting it was the flu or some simple bacterial infection the antibiotic would clear up, Mom and Dad waited over the weekend for the medicine to kick in.

Dad didn't improve at all over the weekend.

My cousin Ricky went to visit my dad, which he often did. Despite being sick, my dad insisted on showing Ricky his large collection of Lionell trains he set up every Christmas. He was setting the trains up on the ping pong table and talked about why he still didn't feel well. Ricky was in medical school but back then we had no idea the pain in his jaw or down his arm were indicators of a heart attack. We all thought he just had the flu. I think things happen for a reason and am glad Ricky was able to spend special time with my dad before he died. Jacob, our Parisian friend, called my dad the week before he died as well. He and Jacob never talked on the phone.

And, while driving to work that week, my dad saw Uncle Marty, which was another weird occurrence. They both pulled over on Meetinghouse Road to have a quick chat. Two more people who were very special to him, like Ricky, were able to see or talk to my dad right before he passed away.

Dad's seizure occurred on that fateful Sunday evening.

"Any news?" I was startled by a familiar voice as I sat quietly beside Mom in the hospital waiting room.

Mom shook her head as I turned to be greeted by Larry, her neighbor. He'd appeared as if from nowhere. He held a Styrofoam cup of sludgy coffee in one hand, obviously from one of the hospital's vending machines.

"Hi, Stacey," he said. "So sorry about your dad."

I thanked him with a weak smile. I'd known Larry since I was a teenager. He lived next to my parents' house and owned a key company. Dad invited him to the Eagles games on occasion, and Larry thought the world of him.

"When your father had his seizure, I went over to Larry's house and asked if he'd drive me to the hospital," Mom explained. "He's stayed with me this whole time."

"I could hardly leave your mother all by herself." Larry smiled.

I was so thankful for him, as I'd gotten there as quickly as possible after Mom had phoned me.

All I knew was my dad had a seizure in his bedroom, which was why Mom had to call an ambulance. Because I thought my dad had only been sick with the flu since Friday, and it was Sunday, I couldn't imagine what might be wrong with him.

"I'm sure he's going to be just fine, Stacey." Larry's well-meaning platitude fell on deaf ears. Distracted, my thoughts were with my dad.

"I called your sisters," my mom had told me the moment I arrived. "I let Tammy know, but I couldn't get hold of Lisa. I called Dr. Haaz too. He's associated with this hospital and a good friend of the family." She and Dad had known Dr. Haaz for as long as I could remember. He'd been to many Berger parties: bat mitzvahs, my wedding, anniversaries. My parents were forever throwing lavish affairs and fun parties to bring friends and family together.

But…

My dad had always said that if anything should happen to him, heart-wise, I needed to call Dr. Nakhjavan immediately. He was a world-renowned cardiologist, and my father had landscaped his mansion in Rydal, a beautiful neighborhood and posh suburb of Philly. In fact, Dr. Nakhjavan had a son, Jeff, who had been in my grade but at Cheltenham, the high school Jon had attended in the town next to mine. A lot of my friends had had crushes on Jeff, and we used to hang out with him and his crew from Cheltenham. As with everyone Dad worked for, Dr. Nakhjavan and he had become close—and Dad loved him; respected and admired the doctor and his career.

Upset, I opened my mouth to confront my mom over her decision to call Dr. Haaz and not Dr. Nakhjavan. But nothing came out. As distressed as I was about Dad and angry at Mom for not even considering calling his chosen doctor, I couldn't muster the inner strength required to stand up to my mother. Even as a grown woman, married with a kid and another on the way, I still couldn't stand up to her!

"The doctor said your father had a heart attack on Thursday," Mom said before I could speak. "That's what all his symptoms were." When he'd come home from work on Friday with a fever and was complaining Thursday night of pain in his jaw (thinking it was his teeth), those were all symptoms of a heart attack.

"They told me he had a rip in his heart muscle," Mom went on. "That's what caused the aches and pains he'd been getting."

At this point, I was still not fearing the worst and expected my healthy, strong father would just need some mild procedure and he would be fine.

Mom continued, "The doctor said his heart has been leaking blood and making it harder and harder for it to pump. That's what caused the seizure." From Thursday night to Sunday night, that little tear bled and bled to the point that the heart was engulfed in blood and could no longer function correctly. As Mom said, that's what caused the seizure.

"Mrs. Berger?" Another voice cut into my thoughts, this one unfamiliar.

"How is he, Doctor?" Mom asked as the tall man wearing a white coat approached the three of us.

The doctor shook his head a little. "I'm afraid your husband is very, very sick."

It was hard for me to believe what I heard—it just didn't register! Dad had always been fit and healthy. *Always*! He paid attention to what he ate, didn't drink or smoke, and exercised even though his job was physical enough. The only time Dad had ever been really sick was when I was a kid, and the Flyers were in the playoffs. He had a nasty dose of the flu or something similar and insisted his friend Dr. Lizerbram, who lived around the corner, come to the house and give him a shot in the butt so he wouldn't miss the game. That was the kind of fan my dad was, just like all the other sports fans in Philadelphia. Dad got the injection and was on his way down to Broad Street and attend the Flyers game!

And yet, despite his healthy habits, there he was in an ER hospital on a Sunday night.

I continued to tell myself he was going to be okay. He would get the very best doctors, and this would all be over soon.

The doctor's eyes flickered away from mine, just long enough for me to notice and figure he was hiding the worst news. "We need to transfer him to

Hahnemann," he told us. "It's a bigger hospital, and much better equipped to treat heart issues such as Barry's."

I wasn't aware the Holy Redeemer Hospital didn't have the best cardiology department, so the doctor's news came as a surprise to me. Could Dad's condition really be *so* bad he must be transferred to another hospital? Again, I thought of Dr. Nakhjavan. What would he suggest? I could have requested they call my father's preferred cardiologist at that juncture but, once again, my inner strength failed me.

After that, we were able to stay with my dad in the hospital emergency room, hold his hand, and talk with him. I could see and hear Dad struggle to breathe. His usually loud, lively voice sounded shallow and weak. Nonetheless, he seemed alert and fully aware of what was going on.

"You're going to have to cancel the trucks at work," Dad instructed my mother. "And put the men on unemployment for now." His words struck a chord deep within me: my father *never* canceled trucks. Even when the weather was too dangerous for him and his crew to work, they worked anyway—and he never, *ever* put his employees on unemployment. In that moment, it crossed my mind that my father knew he was *very* sick.

Dad always worked, no matter what. I told him once that it was 100 degrees outside and asked why he had to go to work and sit in that heat all day. Why couldn't his workers just do the job without him there? His reply was, "If I am not out there working with them, they'll tell me it's too hot to work. If I am there with them, they can't say anything."

I was scared. Not only were they transferring my dad to another hospital, but they were taking him by helicopter. It had all intensified so quickly.

"We're preparing him now. The helicopter is standing by," Dr. Haaz informed us before heading off with my dad.

I drove to Hahnemann Hospital as fast as I could. We were still trying to get in touch with my sisters. Tammy was engaged and living in Atlanta, while Lisa, also engaged, lived in Philly. Lisa was on a date with her fiancé and not answering her phone. When she got home, my poor sister was met with a bunch of missed calls and voicemails from Mom. She finally called back, and Mom let her know the situation with Dad, and she rushed to the hospital as quickly as she could. Tammy made immediate arrangements to fly home to Philadelphia.

In the waiting room, Lisa arrived fifteen, maybe twenty minutes after she talked to Mom. She must have run every red light and broken every speed limit to get there! Shortly after, Aunt Shirley and Uncle Howard turned up and, hot on their heels, Aunt Marleen and Uncle Joel. Aunt Shirley and Uncle Howard had gone to Penn State with my dad and were my parents' best friends. They were very special to me too!

Unconditional Love

Here is an Aunt Shirley story: During Tammy's bat mitzvah, my mom hired a local designer to make us custom black-tie dresses. We all had to wear the same fabric, but we each sat down with the designer, who had a large notepad and pencil, and described to him what we wanted our dresses to look like: long or short, off the shoulder, tight, with a ballroom skirt… Tammy's bat mitzvah was in November, and we all wore our gorgeous new dresses.

In March, four months later, my dad was hosting a big surprise party for my mom's birthday at the Four Seasons. He insisted we wear the same dresses we'd worn four months earlier in front of all the same people. What? That is a fashion no-no! He had spent a crazy amount of money on those dresses and wanted us to get good use out of them. There was no more discussion! I had to call Aunt Shirley. Who else could help? Thank G-d Aunt Shirley was able to change Dad's mind, and we were allowed to get new outfits.

Aunt Marlene and Uncle Joel were also good friends of our family, and Aunt Marlene was a best friend of Mom's. Although I never did see them go out together and the four of them never hung out on a Saturday night. Uncle Joel worked for my parents and came over to the house to help with my dad's landscape plans. There was an "office" in the basement of our house, with a large drafting table, where my Uncle Joel would take a picture of a home and turn that photo into an architectural landscape drawing. This would be the foundation for the "plan" my date would design with trees, bushes and stones. My Aunt Marlene and Uncle Joel are my "cousin" Ricky's parents. Ricky and I have always been close, despite him being Tammy's age. So close that I was a bridesmaid at his wedding. We would grow up and have deep conversations about our parents. Ricky and I saw eye to eye. Our parents were so involved in controlling our lives.

After the cursory greetings, we all sat and waited for news.

Mom told us Hahnemann's entire team of cardiologists were standing by on the hospital roof for Dad's helicopter. The second it landed; they rushed him in for emergency surgery.

I know this isn't okay to say nowadays, not politically correct, but when my mom told me the name of the doctor who would operate on my dad, I could tell he was of Indian descent. "The head cardiologist is an Indian," I told Mom in barely a whisper for fear of offending the very people who were fighting to save my dad's life.

We all knew about Dad's disdain for Indians. He didn't dislike them as a people, he just hated the smell of their cooking. He didn't like working for them because their houses always smelled of the strong, aromatic spices he hated. It was an opinion he chose not to keep a secret from his family.

My first thought was, *we're fucked.* Even more so than before, I wanted Dr Nakhjavan. I wished I had the fortitude to tackle the subject with my mother and *insist* we call him right there and then. But my mind once again played a bunch of possible outcomes to such a confrontation, and none were very pleasant. So, I remained silent.

We looked up with anticipation and dread as a doctor made his way across the waiting room to us. My heart sank, but I was still not prepared for the worst.

"You can come see him for a short while," the young doctor told Mom. "He's awake and asking to see you."

Relief was hardly the word for the emotion that swept through me upon hearing that; I almost cried.

Mom, Lisa, and I followed the doctor from the waiting room along the hallway to where my dad was hooked up to all manner of expensive equipment. "Don't mind all this," he said with a smile—it was one of his forced smiles, I could tell—and he looked exhausted. His eyes dropped to a thick plastic tube snaking out from his chest. "They had to put a catheter in to drain the blood so they can take a look-see at what's going on inside. Then, they'll get me all better." Hope shone in his weary voice.

Then, he said, "I want you to wear this, Stacey." He took off his necklace and handed it to me. It was the beautiful, 24-karat gold Jewish star he *always* wore. I took it from him with trembling hands, convinced he knew something neither he nor the doctors were telling us.

I fastened Dad's necklace around my neck and promised him I would take very good care of it. I later went into the ladies' room and held that Jewish star tight in my hand, maybe trying to get strength from it, maybe expressing how much I loved my dad. Whatever the reason, I didn't want to let go of it.

"I'm afraid it's time for you leave now," the doctor said, breaking the moment. "We need to take Mr. Berger down to surgery." And, with that, he ordered one of the attending nurses to usher the three of us out of Dad's room and out into the hallway to make our own way back to the waiting room.

I sat in that waiting room with Mom, Lisa, and my parents' friends/my "aunts" and "uncles" for what felt like hours. None of us spoke much. I guess we didn't feel like making small talk—we were there to wait.

In the small hours of Monday morning, the chief cardiologist came into the room. Again, my heart leapt into my throat as he made his way toward us.

"Your husband is doing well, Mrs. Berger."

"Can I see him?" Mom asked.

The doctor shook his head. "He is still in surgery," he explained. "We have opened him up and located the tear in his heart muscle. Having looked at it, I can tell you we have two options right now."

I wasn't sure whether to be terrified at the prospect or relieved. Surely, having *two* options to save Dad was a good thing, right?

"The body is very good at mending itself naturally," the doctor continued. "And in cases like your husband's, if we leave him open for a half hour or so, the small tear will most likely heal on its own. Especially with all the blood drained away from around his heart. The second course of action would be to put a patch onto the tear. But with the heart being so sensitive, the patch could cause another heart attack." The doctor paused a moment or two, as if giving us time to soak in what he was telling us. "Of course, both options have their risks, Mrs. Berger. It's important you fully understand that."

"What would *you* do, Doctor?" Mom asked.

"My recommendation would be to have us leave him open for a half hour," he replied. "Then, if there's no further bleeding, we can sew him back up and he can begin his recovery."

Quietly, Mom just nodded and signed the consent form he presented to her.

More than ever, I wished for Dr. Nakhjavan. I felt like I was letting my father down by not insisting.

Then, all we could do was sit and wait again.

It brought me some comfort knowing Dad's body would heal itself given a little time, and a half hour really didn't seem all that long to me. I continued allowing myself to believe my dad was going to be okay.

After longer than thirty minutes—maybe an hour—the cardiologist reappeared. He seemed tired but had a faint smile on his face, which I found reassuring. Lisa, Mom, and me stood up as he approached.

"There is no more bleeding," he told us. "We gave him an extra half hour just to be doubly sure, and it completely stopped of its own accord. Everything is going to be just fine, Mrs. Berger."

"Oh my." Mom almost burst into tears. I don't think I'd ever seen her look so happy. "Thank you so much, Doctor. We shall send you and your family away for a week's vacation for saving my husband! Anywhere in the world you want to go."

"There really is no need—"

"Please…" Mom interrupted. "You saved my husband's life. It's the very least we can do!"

Although he didn't know how persistent my mom could be, I think the cardiologist understood when to graciously smile and say thank you.

We were all elated! After waiting so long for some good news about Dad's prognosis, we had finally received it!

"He's going to be okay, Mom," I said, my voice about to crack. I felt such a sense of relief I thought I was going to cry.

Mom immediately called Tammy, who was just about to get on her plane. "He's going to be ok, Tammy!" she blurted out the second my sister picked up. Lisa and I listened too!

"That's *awesome*!" Tammy sounded on the verge of tears. "Are you *sure*?"

"The chief cardiologist told us himself," Mom explained. "He said Daddy's heart is repairing itself, and he's on the way to making a full recovery."

"Have you seen him?" Tammy asked.

"Yeah, but he was asleep." Mom, Lisa, and I had snuck a peek at Dad in the recovery room. He was hooked up to even more tubes, wires, and monitors than he had been when we had gotten to speak with him earlier. He had looked peaceful, though.

"I hope he's awake when I get there!" Tammy sighed. "I'll be with you in a few hours."

We hadn't moved from the waiting room all night and were hungry. It had been a long, long night, and we were all exhausted. Nonetheless, eating something, even hospital cafeteria food, sounded like a great idea. It also meant we could finally leave the waiting room.

My dad was going to be okay.

We trooped down to the cafeteria and, although the food was pretty much as we'd expected for early-morning hospital fare, we all felt a heck of a lot better after getting some of it inside us.

Before returning to the waiting room, I ducked into the bathroom again, where I clutched my dad's necklace tight and said a couple of prayers, even though I wasn't normally the type to pray.

This time, as we sat in the waiting room, we were filled with relief and happiness that Dad was going to be okay. After a while, the chief cardiologist came back. Thinking he was there to let us know Dad was awake and ready to receive visitors, we jumped up to greet him.

In my excitement, I hadn't noticed the slowness in the surgeon's step and the downturn of his eyes. It was as if he couldn't quite bear to look at us all standing there eager to see Dad.

"Could you come with me, please?" the surgeon said quietly to Mom, Lisa, and me. He held out an arm to direct us toward a smaller side room. The sign on the door read, *Private*.

As we made our way toward the door, a terrible gnawing sensation grew in the pit of my stomach. During our night, I'd watched others going into that room, and they always came out upset and crying. I think every hospital has a smaller room such as that one: a tiny sanctuary away from the rest of the friends and relatives waiting for good news of their loved ones, a place where good news simply didn't happen.

More than anything in the whole wide world, I didn't want to go into that room!

No, I am not going into that room!

He must have the wrong family…

The cardiologist switched on the light and closed the door behind us. In an instant, I felt scared and terribly alone.

"I'm so sorry, Mrs. Berger." He spoke softly, gently to my mother, his eyes settling upon hers. "I'm afraid your husband had another heart attack in the recovery room. A very serious one."

"No…" was all mom could manage to say.

My heart sank.

"We did everything we could to save him, but I'm afraid we just couldn't. The damage to his heart was devastating. He stopped breathing for so long that, even if we had managed to revive him, he could effectively be brain dead. He passed away a few minutes ago."

Mom burst into tears and collapsed into Lisa's arms. My sister began wailing too, and the pair of them sobbed hysterically. My heart broke. They sat together on a small, padded bench, and I collapsed in a chair opposite. Even though I was pregnant and incredibly hormonal, I was too shocked to cry; my mind and emotions were numb. All I could feel was a detached sensation of denial.

Dad *couldn't* be gone.

It just wasn't possible.

The door to that awful, small room opened. Mom and Lisa were too wrapped up in their grief to register we had a visitor, but I turned to greet him. "Hello." I shook the priest's hand.

"I'll leave you alone," the cardiologist whispered. His work was done. "If you need me or have any questions, please have one of the nurses page me." With that, he was gone.

The priest walked into that small cubby hole of a room and offered his condolences. "I'm so sorry for your loss. I know this is a difficult time for you all."

My mom and sister sobered and stood with tear-stained faces, staring at the priest. He was a wonderful man and spent a long time talking with us, offering words of comfort, listening as we shared our grief. Mom and Lisa cried through most of it, hysterically so, but I just sat in that uncomfortable chair and felt nothing. After the priest had talked to us for some time, somewhere in the conversation we mentioned being Jewish. The priest was surprised and embarrassed. He said he would get a rabbi for us right away.

"If you'd prefer a rabbi, I can organize one to come see you. Nobody told me you were Jewish." The poor man looked genuinely uncomfortable.

"No," we reassured him. "We want you. We *like* you!"

That seemed to alleviate the awkward situation. I have no idea why a specific religion should ever matter under those circumstances; all we needed was someone to comfort us and listen to us in our hour of need. Also, we didn't want to start over with someone else, and we genuinely *liked* him. Not one of us cared he was a priest and not a rabbi—he was the one who had come to soothe my father's newly bereaved family.

"Is there anyone you need me to call for you?" he asked as he stood to leave.

"My husband's parents." Through her sniffles, Mom sounded terribly cold. Had I not known better, I'd have assumed she was too upset to call my grandparents and tell them the terrible news about losing *another* son.

But I did know better. Mom's coldhearted reply was because she didn't *want* to call them. At that time, I *still* believed everything my parents told me about my grandparents and didn't see my mom's reply as insensitive. I was possibly in shock she wanted the priest to call them instead. It was unbelievable, but I was still my mom's protector and kept silent. I wish I was as strong then as I am today because I really should have called my grandparents myself! How horrible it must have been for them to receive such news from a stranger.

Father O'Malley looked a little taken aback. "Are you sure you don't want to do that yourself? Perhaps if you wait a little while…"

Mom shook her head. The priest had no idea of the bad blood festering between my mother and her husband's parents. "I'd rather you do it," she said. "I can give you, their number."

With a compliant nod, he jotted down my grandparents' contact information onto a slip of paper and sat back down to call them.

Shortly afterward, with my grandparents on their way to the hospital, a nurse came to collect Mom, Lisa, and me.

"You can come see him now. If you're up to it," the nurse told us. "Take your time, though."

Before going in to see Dad, I called Jon and asked him to get to the hospital as quickly as he possibly could. I explained what had happened and told him I needed him with me. "I called Joan," I added. "She's going to come over and take care of Josh. He's too young for all of this. I think it's best he stays home."

"Sure." Jon's voice sounded flat, deflated. He loved Dad deeply, and I knew he'd be devastated to lose him.

Joan told me later Jon had gone outside into our backyard that morning and screamed out his grief at the top of his lungs.

I felt especially bad for my sister Tammy. She'd thought Dad was going to be okay and make a full recovery just before she stepped onto her airplane from Atlanta. I can't begin to describe just how crushed my sister was when she arrived at the hospital excited to see Dad looking well after his health scare, only to be told he had passed away.

After Jon, I called my best friends Andy and Maddie. I had to call Maddie from the hospital payphone because my cell battery had died. I told them the bad news and asked if they'd come to the hospital to be with me. I needed to be surrounded by friends at that awful time. It was especially weird because, when I called Maddie earlier after the cardiologist had said Dad was going to be fine, Maddie acted as if she knew he wouldn't be. She somehow had psychic abilities!

Andy arrived at the hospital before my husband. As he walked out of the elevator, I was so happy to see him and gave him the biggest hug. For the first time since receiving the traumatizing news from the cardiologist, I allowed myself to cry.

Mom-mom and Pop-pop arrived at almost the same time as Jon. I was cried out by then and had returned to my shocked, numb state. Immediately, as my grandparents entered, I felt the atmosphere switch from one of shared grief among those of us who'd been there all night to one of frosty resentment. My mother flatly refused to acknowledge my poor grandparents, let alone force herself to speak to them. I can't imagine what they must have been going through, having just tragically lost *another* son, only to be shunned by his wife.

I'm ashamed to admit I, too, was not nice to Mom-mom and Pop-pop. Even in grief, I felt obliged to stand in line with Mom's stance. She had made it clear in that small room she didn't want to even *speak* to my grandparents. I would never, ever think of going against her and automatically followed her lead.

Looking back, ashamed is not a strong enough word for how I feel. I would have been nicer to a stranger who was grieving. But in the shock of losing my dad and the turmoil my family had gone through for years, I stood by Mom, protecting and defending her from anything that may hurt her.

Everyone in my family was mean to my grandparents at the hospital, despite the heartbreaking loss they'd just endured. From the day my dad died, Mom blamed my grandparents for his premature death: because of all the ill-feeling between them, *they* had killed him.

After a while, we all made our way back to my parents' house. The drive seemed to last forever, even though I took a few shortcuts and arrived well ahead of everyone else. For the first time in my life, I dreaded going into my old childhood home. Dad wouldn't be there, and he was the one who always lit the place up for me, who made me feel so special.

The first thing I saw as I stepped inside the hallway was my dad's work boots. We had a little ledge off the living room into the foyer, where he stored all his work clothes and landscaping plans, neatly rolled up and secured with a rubber band. Seeing his boots, overalls, and plans laying there, as if waiting patiently for him to come back home, overwhelmed me with emotion. I wanted to cry again, to let out my grief and rage at losing my precious father so soon. We should have had so many more years together. He should have had the opportunity to welcome his second grandchild into the world and build a relationship with her and Josh

I swallowed down the looming tears and decided it would be for the best if I moved Dad's things out of the way so my mom wouldn't have to see them too. I picked up the boots, overalls, and plans and carried them down into the basement. There, I laid them carefully on one of his old workbenches. It felt like saying goodbye.

The phone in the basement rang, startling me. "Hello, Stacey?"

"Hi." I recognized the voice. It was Esteen Wells from New Jersey.

"Is it true? Is it true? Is Barry gone?" Mrs. Wells sounded like she'd been sobbing. Nobody else had even returned from the hospital, and we were already getting calls. I guess the old Jewish grapevine had been busy, and word of Barry Berger's passing had spread like wildfire. Everyone who knew Dad loved him and would miss him terribly.

Chapter Thirty-One:
Saying Goodbye

> *I miss my dad. The loss of your father no matter how old you are changes your life forever. Your dad is your protector who keeps you safe and secure. You never really get over the loss, you learn to live with it, and he is never far away from your thoughts.*
> —Afreen Hyder, "Selflove"

In keeping with Jewish tradition, Dad's funeral was held within forty-eight hours of his passing. After that, the Shiva process began, along with our chance to truly mourn. Many visitors came to pay their respects over the following days.

Dad's funeral, predictably, was a huge event. So many people from all over the country (and beyond!) wanted to say their final farewells to my wonderful dad, Barry Berger! After the absolute chaos of organizing the myriad mourners at Uncle Kenny and Aunt Aviva's funeral, I thought I'd be prepared for anything. We used Goldstein's again, the biggest Jewish funeral directors in Philadelphia, and they told us that both Dad's and Uncle Kenny's funerals were by far the biggest they had ever arranged in all their years of business.

It wasn't so much the special friends and family members who formed a long, orderly line outside the funeral home, it was the number of ordinary, everyday folks whose lives had been touched in some small way by my father that truly moved me. One guy, no more than twenty or twenty-one, introduced himself to me and said, "I worked at the gas station where your dad used to fill up his work trucks. He was one hell of a guy." Countless restaurant waitresses and maître ds filed in to say goodbye. Betty the head waitress and Jack the maître d' from Dad's all-time favorite restaurant The Blue Bell Inn came to the house for Shiva as well! It was amazing to see how much my father had affected people's lives—not just close friends and business associates but everyone he'd ever encountered. Eddie Bruce, the band leader, came to honor my dad too! My dad brought joy and light everywhere he went, (and sometimes his temper) and all who'd ever known him were united in the grief of his passing.

Jacob and Martine flew across the world from Paris. They were devastated at the news and insisted upon dropping everything to get to Philadelphia. Jacob didn't even wait in the receiving line at the funeral home. I remember watching him skipping the line, walking quickly along the side wall, and right up to the front to see my mom. Uncle Paul and my cousin Todd drove all the way from Florida, as they didn't want to wait to make travel plans at the airport. They just got in the car and drove straight to our house. My cousins Ricky and Casey flew in from Arkansas too!

I wanted Ricky to be a pallbearer, but my mom said it wouldn't be fair to his brother Gary. But Gary wasn't close with my dad like Ricky was. I expressed my feelings to my mom and convinced her to choose Ricky.

Mom, my sisters, and I each wrote a eulogy for Dad. Lisa, Tammy, and I asked the rabbi to read ours; none of us were confident we'd get through it without breaking down. Mom read hers to the congregation with grace and strength. She said he was her king, and she was his queen. As a child, even when they fought, I always felt the love between my parents. That love was the foundation of our family.

I remember sitting on the steps in my townhouse attempting to write a fitting eulogy for my dad. I was still in shock, of course. It seemed surreal, like it really wasn't happening.

But it was.

I wrote about Josh and how sad it was he wouldn't know Dad as a papa, about the baby in my belly who I was going to name after him, and about how the Flyers were doing. I loved Dad with all my heart, and I would miss him every single day of my life. I promised I would *take care of Mommy and make sure everything was all right.*

Some things never change. Even as a grown adult with a family of my own, I still felt it was my duty to organize things and make sure everything and everybody was okay. I worried so much about my mom, made sure she was eating, and checked on her as soon as I woke up!

After the service, two different people—strangers—approached me to say they wished *their* daughters loved them as much as my sisters and I obviously loved my dad, and they'd work hard to be better fathers to their own children. It was so cool that Dad had influenced complete strangers. Through our profound sadness, I was proud to show everyone how much my sisters and I loved him.

After the funeral, the family went back to the house, and our seven days of Shiva began. Shiva is a different mourning process for immediate family members—children, spouses, siblings—and has its own traditions. The rabbi gave me, as the daughter, a pin, which I had to wear for thirty days. How many days you must wear the pin depends on the loss, whether you are a spouse, child, or parent. The pin was attached to a black ribbon, which I ripped, according to Jewish tradition. Just like after the crash, when my aunt's family ripped their clothes, the torn ribbon, worn over my chest, symbolized my broken heart. I still have my pin in my jewelry box. I will *never* throw it out. Both Lisa and Tammy wore pins and ripped ribbons too, as we were united in our grief.

During the seven days we sat for Shiva, a lot of the mourners, many of them my family and friends, went out drinking and smoking to numb their pain. I wished I could leave and hang out with them, but I was pregnant, so I had to stay in the house with all the well-wishers. I developed an obsession with Jewish apple cake, which people brought to the house in huge quantities. For the uninitiated, it's very similar to banana bread—and incredibly delicious!

It is an old Jewish custom during Shiva for friends, family, and neighbors to prepare and bring over food for the mourners to eat. Since Dad had been so well-loved and popular, we were inundated with Shiva baskets containing every conceivable variety of food! So much so, Mom lined the leftovers up on the ledge by the front door—the one Dad had always used for his work clothes and landscaping plans—and gave them away to charity. I wanted to eat absolutely *everything* on that ledge. It all looked and smelled divine. But since food was not to be taken from a Shiva house, as much as I wanted to devour it or take it home for Jon and Josh, I simply could not.

We all deal with grief in our own ways, I understand that. After Dad passed, I retreated into myself and kept busy during Shiva by making sure everything and everybody was okay. I made sure guests' coats were hung up on the coat racks we rented, regularly checked on Mom, cleaned up dirty plates and cups when people were done eating, and then checked on my mom again. Did she need something to eat? A drink? A hug? Of course, my own heart was broken—I didn't need the torn ribbon to show that—but I buried my emotions deep down so I could take care of everyone else.

Lisa and Tammy, on the other hand, expressed their grief by sitting together on the love seat in Mom's living room and crying together. The whole time. Day and night.

Well, that's how it seemed like to me.

Unconditional Love

My sisters' actions separated us. Not only because they didn't lift a finger to help during the entire seven days—they assumed *I'd* be the one to handle everything as usual—but it seemed people thought they loved Dad more than I did because I wasn't as outwardly upset as they were. I understood my sisters were grieving for their father, which is a unique kind of grief all by itself, but we experienced it differently. For example, my sisters both took all their pictures of my dad down because it upset them too much to see him. I *loved* to keep all his pictures around me and never put them away. People grieve, each in their own way —I learned that from my dad's passing. The three of us had lost the same person, but our reactions weren't the same. I was able to say, "When Daddy died…" much sooner than they were. I recall talking with my sisters and saying, "daddy died" and they both acted as if those words made them *so* uncomfortable, looking at each other and then down at the floor. I didn't realize that hearing those words upset them so much and made a note to myself to never say that to them again.

I focused on making Shiva go smoothly for everyone and confirming my mother was okay and eating. She never ate much. I dutifully heaped her plate with the delicious, donated food and watched her pick at it. She had a sparrow's appetite, which was understandable under the circumstances, but at least she was eating *something*.

I talked to as many folks as I could about Dad. Everyone had such wonderful stories to tell about him, and it was cathartic to hear them all and exchange a few of my own. It felt comforting to be surrounded by so many good people who loved my dad. It was almost like having him around. I loved to hear everyone's memories; I couldn't get enough.

Mom-mom and Pop-pop visited the house every day. Enveloped in their own grief, they arrived first thing in the morning and sat quietly on the same love seat in the den until nightfall. Their friends and family visited and spent time with them. But nobody in my family talked to them, no one offered to comfort them, throughout the entire seven days. I didn't because I was afraid of upsetting my mother. In fact, I assured her I wouldn't let them get anywhere near her. There I was again, protecting her. Those poor people mourned the loss of their second son, surrounded by others but completely ignored by my family.

I was oblivious to my grandparents' predicament. My priority was to shelter Mom from them, to defend her just as I used to defend Dad, and to block them from approaching her. Indoctrinated, I viewed Mom-mom and Pop-pop as the enemy, but deep down I didn't believe mom's rhetoric that the stress they caused had been instrumental in Dad's death.

Unconditional Love

Many years later, long after I saw things for how they really were, I apologized to my grandparents for how I treated them during their lonely days of Shiva. I was totally ashamed by my behavior.

While Lisa and Tammy lived at my parents' house with Mom throughout Shiva—and continued to do so for two or three months afterwards—I returned home each evening to be with my own family. I was married, pregnant, and had a small child who needed me. In many ways, it was a relief for me to be out of Mom's house and away from all that grief, though I did miss all the happy reminiscences about Dad.

Jacob and Martine stayed with Mom the whole week too. It's at times like that when you learn who your real friends are, and I know Mom was grateful to have them around.

During Shiva, I found myself talking to Jimmy Hoffman and his wife Jody. He was a builder my dad worked with on many occasions over the years. In fact, Dad had worked with Jimmy's father long before Jimmy took over the family business, so it was a long and fruitful relationship!

"It was only a week ago when I last saw your father," Jody told me with a tear welling in her eye. "I came home one day, and he'd planted trees all down one side of the house. It was a lovely surprise, and they were all so beautiful. Then he popped by to tell me he'd be bringing a lilac tree to finish off that side of the house. He knew lilacs are my favorite."

That was just the sort of thing my dad would do. Go to a customer or friends' house and surprise them with a new bush or tree. And remembering her love of lilacs… Most likely, Jimmy had nonchalantly shared that information, and Dad had stored it away in his memory because he relished doing nice things for others.

Later, I repeated Jody's story to my mom and suggested we send her over a lilac tree. Mom's answer gave me my first inklings of confusion over my family and how we functioned. In fact, her reply shocked me. I remember coming down the steps from upstairs into the kitchen and suggesting we send the lilac tree to the Hoffmans.

"And why would we do that?" She seemed genuinely nonplussed by the notion.

"Because it's what Daddy would have wanted us to do. It's what *he* would have done." I didn't think I needed to explain, but I did anyway.

"Do you have any idea how much lilac trees cost?" Her retort was cutting.

Of course I had no idea how much lilac trees cost, and I got the impression Mom didn't either. But it wasn't about money. We could certainly afford a damn tree for an old work associate of Dad's.

During that conversation with Mom, doubts and realizations began to creep into my mind: perhaps the Berger family hadn't been so perfect after all.

Unconditional Love

I had been wearing the necklace Dad gave me since he put it into my hand the last time I saw him alive in the hospital. It hadn't left my neck for a single second. At the time, it was the most precious thing I had, a final memory of my beloved father. It was like having a piece of him with me. When putting Josh in his crib, the necklace would dangle from my neck and Josh would always try to grab it, to catch it moving in the air. Every night, as he grabbed the necklace, tears would spring to my eyes. I clutched the Jewish star tight and thought of how much I loved my dad and how much I already missed him.

But, a few days into Shiva, my mom told me I had to share the necklace with my sisters. I was upset at the idea of taking it off. But I obediently handed it over to Lisa so she would have her chance to wear it. If only I'd been strong enough then to stand up to her and say *no*. Dad had given it to me because he wanted *me* to have it. It broke my heart to hand Dad's necklace over, and I'm so angry I was too much under the family's spell to argue.

Eventually, we decided to make a mold of Dad's charm and have the original broken into three equal parts, for my sisters and me. We each decided what to engrave on the back of our piece. Of course, Lisa and Tammy chose the same thing, while I wrote something different. However, when we went to the jeweler to pick them up, there were three pieces, but one was half and the other two were each a quarter. Which section belonged to who was determined by what was written on the back.

We turned the bigger piece around to find "My Daddy" —that was mine! My sisters received the two smaller pieces.

Mom would later use the mold to make a replica of the pendant to present to Josh at his bar mitzvah. When he lost it ten years later, Mom gave me the mold to order a replacement. I guess she thought she'd already paid for one and wasn't going to pay for another. I thought it was weird she wouldn't want to keep the mold for herself or her other grandchildren or as a memento.

At Christmas time, in the malls, you can get any portrait you like printed onto a mug. One year, I gave my dad a mug with Josh's baby picture on it. After he died, my mom gave me back the mug; she didn't even want to have it in her house. To this day, I don't understand her motivation. You have the cutest image of your grandson on one side, and on the other it reads "Best Grandpa," and you don't want to keep it? It was another one of those things that didn't make sense to me.

Chapter Thirty-Two:
A New Normal

We must let go of the life we have planned, so as to accept the one that is waiting for us.

—Joseph Campbell

Once Shiva was over, the mourners and well-wishers returned to their own lives. Jacob and Martine left for the airport with a tearful farewell; with Dad gone, we knew things would never be the same again.

We'd gotten used to having a house filled with people and more donated food than we could possibly eat, and it seemed strange without the others, although Mom did receive the occasional visitor who'd pop round to make sure she was holding up. Tammy and Lisa hung around, providing company for Mom, but that was it. Even I went back to my life and prepared for the imminent birth of my second child.

On occasion, Mom, Lisa, Tammy, and I ventured out to lunch or the mall, and I felt like everyone was looking at us. I imagined them whispering, "Their dad just died," and it was an uncomfortable sensation. I started reading books about grieving. I bought as many as I could and devoured them to figure out what I should feel and how to deal with it.

I learned that, if someone is sick with a disease or has had surgery, people can see something visible straightaway, understand something is wrong, and react accordingly with sympathy and compassion. However, with grief, nothing is visible, no sickly pallor, no bandages, no wheelchair, and no one can tell how much you're hurting inside. They simply don't know what you're going through.

In the months following Dad's passing, we all tried to move on with life. We couldn't mourn Dad forever, right?

Vowing to look after Mom, I went out of my way to be there for her. I begged my husband to call her and check on her, to offer to go over and fix a lightbulb, but he wouldn't. He didn't like her and wasn't going to help her. But Lisa's boyfriend stopped by all the time, trying to assist her.

When my Uncle Howard's mother died not too long after my dad, I didn't like the thought of my mom going to the funeral alone. I insisted on joining her, even though I was pregnant and uncomfortable. Lisa and Tammy were noticeably absent. They'd not even *offered* to attend. Nor did I suggest it to them. It was just the way things were.

There is an old Jewish custom—or superstition, if you prefer—that dictates a pregnant woman is not permitted in a cemetery. It has something to do with not mixing new life with death, but nonetheless I stood by Mom's side throughout the whole thing. I honestly felt I *had* to go with her, even though I now think, *why couldn't my sisters do that?* That thought didn't cross my mind at the time. My duty seemed normal to me, given the dynamics of my family. My priority was supporting my mother like I'd promised Dad I would.

Not too long after, my mom told me my aunt Marcy and uncle Paul were flying in from Boca, Florida, to Atlantic City, and Uncle Howard and Aunt Shirley were meeting them there. These were some of my parents' best friends. Mom was also going to go down the shore to see with them.

I didn't like the thought of Mom driving down the shore alone, parking the car in the garage alone, and walking into our apartment alone. I insisted on going with her. I told her I didn't want to go out with her and my aunts and uncles and would stay in the apartment and watch a movie or read a book. I just didn't want her to come home to an empty apartment.

And that was precisely what I did.

Mom and I took long walks on the boardwalk while we were down there and talked about moving forward without Dad. We also got Steele's fudge and some hot roasted peanuts.

"I'm always going to be there for you, Mom," I said. "I know things have been difficult for you with Dad gone. All I want is for you to be happy." I wanted to comfort her in every way I could think of, but it didn't feel like she appreciated my care. It was confusing and unfamiliar.

I planned to stick to the promise I'd made to my dad to take care of Mom's wellbeing, but something had switched inside her. She'd always been controlling, demanding, and stubborn, but after Dad died, those traits became more pronounced.

For starters, she cancelled the family's Eagles tickets! I never got to see another Eagles game in our seats again—the seats in which Dad, Lisa, and I had shared so many exciting times. Deep down, I knew Dad would have wanted us to keep those season tickets forever, to keep those happy family memories alive. I was upset, but accepted Mom's decision. I would never dare disagree or argue with her. I figured she must have had a good reason.

I was glad she kept the Flyers tickets, though. I attended as many games as I was able to until, a few years later, Mom cancelled those too.

Wait—no more Flyers games?

Although I remained silent once again, I struggled to understand Mom's reasoning. It wasn't because she couldn't afford to keep the tickets—Dad had left her more than enough—so it just came across as mean-spirited to me. She explained we weren't going to enough games, and she was left with tickets she couldn't sell. But I knew other people sold ten-game packages, so I figured she could have sold the entire season and kept those tickets until one of us could start paying for them. Or Lisa and I could have each gotten ten games and Mom could have sold the rest. It seemed like an awful loss to me, another cracking memory of my childhood.

At one point, I asked Mom if Jon could wear Dad's Rolex watch. Both my sisters were unmarried, with boyfriends who had never met Dad. I wanted Jon to wear it and pass it to Josh when he was old enough. I couldn't think of anyone else who deserved it.

"No, Stacey." Mom was adamant. "I just couldn't bear to see someone else wearing it." She told me she was going to put it in the safety deposit box at the bank.

I was finally beginning to summon the strength to say what I was really thinking to her. I said, "I don't think Daddy would want it locked away in the bank." In fact, I *knew* damn well he wouldn't. Why should it sit in a bank?

"I just can't, Stacey. It would break my heart to have to look at your father's watch again." And that was it; her decision was made. She wasn't emotional or crying—it was just a matter of fact that she couldn't bear to look at the watch on someone else's wrist and would keep it locked away in the bank.

Knowing I was beaten, I let the subject drop. Dad's beautiful watch, the one that meant so much to me, sat in the safety deposit box for another twenty-three years until Tammy asked for it. I received a group text from Tammy to me and Lisa, asking if either of us objected to her wearing Dad's Rolex. What was there to say? Mom was more than happy to give it to Tammy. She went to the bank and retrieved the Rolex and all my dad's other jewelry to give to my sisters and me.

There were diamond pinky rings, a solid gold dress watch, and some of my mother's own jewelry she would let us share, including *her* Rolex.

In the end, Tammy got Dad's Rolex and Lisa got Mom's. It had been so many years after Dad's passing and I wasn't getting along with them, so I didn't argue, and I tried to not care.

I received Dad's pinky ring which fit perfectly on my ring finger. Since I was divorced by then, wearing his ring on that finger made me so happy. I have never taken it off since that day. I wish I'd had the chance to wear it over the past twenty-three years, but my mom kept everything under lock and key at the bank and didn't want to share anything until *she* decided the time was right.

When my dad died, I questioned what would happen to the nursery. The nursery was in Warminster not far from where I lived. As you pulled up to the extra wide driveway, to the left stood a single-family home where Dad's foreman and his family lived. The Barry's Green Thumb trucks were parked in front of a big garage. My dad was so proud of the nursery, with its perfect irrigation systems and rows and rows of colorful bushes and trees.

I asked my mom what she was going to do with the nursery, and her plan was to sell it. Okay, fine. But nobody was interested in buying it, and she had to auction it off. I figured she wouldn't get much and knew Dad wouldn't want it torn down. The nursery was his legacy, his pride and joy.

I thought it would be nice to sell it to some other landscaper who would really appreciate and take care of it. I knew two boys from Cheltenham who had a thriving landscaping business and suggested we ask them if they would be interested in it. She shut me down immediately and called my idea ridiculous.

Whatever she got for selling the nursery at auction, I will never know. But every year for the next two decades, I would drive by the nursery, and it was still there, *Barry's Green Thumb* sign on the garage, an unlived in, unkept home, and overgrown grass and weeds filling the property. It wasn't until right before Covid that I drove by, and the nursery was gone. They had built a new development of detached homes on the property. At least it wasn't ugly and dirty anymore, but what a waste to sit there for almost twenty years: a perfectly arranged nursery with a single-family home someone could have benefited from. I truly believe that was what my dad would have wanted.

Chapter Thirty-Three:
My Bari

I went into labor with my daughter Bari, at 6:00 a.m. on September 28, 1998. My father-in-law dashed to our house to stay with Josh, and Mom met Jon and me at the hospital. It was only six months after my dad died and I missed him extra on that day.

The whole thing was an ordeal. I kept asking for painkillers in the emergency room, but the nurses had to wait for my doctor's approval. Personally, I didn't care if they went down to North Philly and got me the good drugs—I would have taken anything at that point! My husband and mom stayed with me, and my gynecologist, Dr. Hoffman, said to me mid-labor, "Your dad is looking over you, Stacey, and he's *really* proud of you." Those words got me through the worst of it. You see, Dr. Hoffman was special to me. When he heard of my dad's passing, he called my mom's house asking for me during Shivah. That meant so much to me. And then, Bari's heart stopped beating somewhere in the middle of all my pushing and screaming because the umbilical cord was wrapped around her little neck.

Acting quickly, the gynecologist and his team delivered just my daughter's head so they could cut the cord and allow her to breathe—and all this without painkillers for me! To make things worse, they had just put in the epidural and it hadn't had time to work its magic. Then they delivered the rest of Bari's, which thankfully went without further mishap—but they had to use forceps again!

And there she was!

Unconditional Love

I knew in my heart Dr. Hoffman had been right: Dad *was* proud of me, but I missed him so much. His absence was palpable, and I felt so empty.

As Jews, we name our children after people who have passed away. This was the perfect way for me to honor Dad and still have him with me. I named my daughter Bari Leigh, from my dad's name—Barry Lee. She was my princess to complement Josh, my prince.

Jewish boys have the bris and girls have a baby naming ceremony. We had Bari's at the synagogue. Just as I wrapped Bari in Dad's tallit (the fringed shawl used for prayer) for her baby naming.

There was a celebration afterward, which Mom took charge of organizing. Josh's baby party, his Pidyon Haben, had been held at the exclusive Pyramid Club in the center of Philadelphia, complete with live band, sumptuous food, and a multitude of guests—a full-blown affair. I'd expected Mom to carry on our tradition of going all out with our parties, but she had other ideas. She arranged for a quiet luncheon after the service, in the back room of the synagogue for a handful of relatives and close friends. Instead of the live band Dad had booked for Josh's party, we had an elderly man playing the organ. It was exactly the type of party my dad hated: no music, all the tables close together, and no dancing.

It was a boring contrast to what I'd grown up with.

But it was what Mom had wanted. She was paying, and she was used to getting her way by then, even on someone else's special day!

When she told me they would be serving wine, I was afraid to suggest what I really wanted mimosas and Bloody Mary's. But Mom insisted on wine.

I *hate* wine. I thought Bloody Mary's and mimosas would be a lot more fun and, since it was a brunch, more appropriate. I finally got up the courage to ask again, a second time, if we could have the cocktails instead. Mom treated me like I was acting like a spoiled child. She made me feel like I had the absolute nerve for asking! Her response chilled me and made me uncomfortable.

Mom served wine, no cocktails.

Andy and I slipped out of the party for a short while to get high and give me time to calm down. When Dad was around, Mom would have asked me, or we would have talked about what I wanted for the party. But she'd changed; it all had to be *her* way, and she expected me to show appreciation. I fell in line, but it didn't feel the same. She was cold and unfamiliar to me.

Chapter Thirty-Four:
What's Going On?

> *An enmeshed family can maintain an illusion of love and stability as long as no one attempts to separate and as long as everyone follows the family rules.*
>
> —Susan Forward

When Mom began dating, I accepted the stark fact that life was moving on without my dad. I was happy for her because I didn't want her to be alone. She was still young, beautiful, smart, and no doubt had plenty of good years left in her, so it made sense for her to seek out the company of men.

One of her early male friends—a nice, soft-spoken type—seemed like a good fit for Mom. They went to Florida together and stayed in a hotel where Mom had to make her own coffee in the room in the morning. *There was no room service.* No coffee delivered in an antique silver teapot with a hot croissant just like my mom loved. It was so different, but I supposed Mom really liked the guy.

At one point, though, she decided to take him to visit Dad's grave, which struck me as odd. I felt immediately protective of my dad. Mom's new man certainly didn't belong there!

Thankfully, she never went again, with or without another man. I was the only one who visited Dad's grave, once a year on Father's Day, which had always been a very special day for me. When driving into the cemetery, you were greeted by people who gave out roses—they were there every year. I never knew what to do at the cemetery; I just wanted to spend time with Dad. Every year, I took a big roll of paper towels, cleaning products, and some flowers. I made sure he was perfectly clean and shiny—Mr. Clean's Magic Erasers were the best! —and planted the pretty flowers at the base of the stone. Nobody in my family ever went to see Dad's grave—not my sisters and not even my mom. Every year though, they thanked me for going.

One year, I got the urge to visit Dad on a day other than Father's Day and clean him up. So, I did. I drove over and made him sparkle and planted beautiful orange flowers at the bottom of the stone. A few days later, my Pop-pop died. The entire family and Pop-pop's friends arrived at the same cemetery as Dad's and, according to Jewish tradition, visited other loved ones and placed a rock on top of their stones. When everybody paid their respects to my dad, he was all clean and looking spiffy with fresh blooms. The incident freaks me out today. I feel like Dad had said to me, "You'd better get over there and clean me up. People will be coming soon."

Shortly after, Mom decided to take me and my sisters to Florida to get away for a little. We stayed at the Breakers at Palm Beach for a long weekend. The Breakers is one of America's most iconic resorts, a historic renaissance style luxury hotel situated on 140 acres of oceanfront property. My parents went to the Breakers sometimes in the winter when my dad wasn't working and would stay two or three weeks. We also went as a family a couple times, including one year for New Year's Eve. Although it was a beautiful place and a welcome break, it was also the location where I experienced another bout of confusion regarding my family. You might even call it an epiphany.

On our first night at the Breakers, Mom asked if any of us wanted grapefruit and/or cantaloupe from room service first thing the following morning. What? That was weird. We never ordered fruit in the morning. The other three wanted to get up early and go for a walk, but I did not. I wanted to sleep late. I had a baby and a toddler at home, so it was heaven to be able to get some undisturbed sleep. While I was sleeping late, they all got up, ate their fruit, and went on their walk. Going for an early morning stroll was something we never, ever did as a family. Normally, when we were all awake, we would decide together what we were going to do for breakfast.

I woke up just as they returned, and I was hungry. "What do you guys want to do for breakfast?" I asked as I crawled out of my comfy bed.

"We already ate before our walk," Mom told me.

I sat, confused. Was the grapefruit and melon their breakfast, and they weren't going to eat again until lunch? Where did that leave me? We *always* went out for breakfast. So, I ordered room service. Things weren't the same.

Unconditional Love

A little later that morning, on the first day, Tammy had a huge fight with her fiancé back in Atlanta. She was on the phone with him for what seemed like the whole afternoon and well into the evening. At that time, we didn't have cell phones like we do today, and it was very expensive to call long distance on a hotel phone. It cost a fortune! Tammy was in the room all day on the line, and eventually the sun started to go down. In my mind, it was time to shower and go out for dinner.

I watched the clock as it got later and later, my stomach growling, desperately waiting for my sister to finish her argument and hang up so we could all go eat. It didn't appear that anyone else was hungry or cared about food, but the thought of going to a restaurant alone was unheard of—we *always* had to go together!

7:00 came and went, as did 8:00.

Starving, I bid my time until 9:00, which finally signaled the end of Tammy's phone call, before making my way into the other room. There, Tammy's drama had Mom and Lisa enthralled.

I know it sounds crazy, but I felt *nervous*. "I'm hungry," I announced. "And if we wait much longer, by the time you all shower and get ready, we'll be eating dinner at ten o'clock."

I imagined my mom and sisters would be thinking, *how can you worry about eating when Tammy is so upset?* I felt like the naughty, plump little girl I used to be, who loved food just a little too much.

But nobody answered me, so I walked away and considered what to do. "I'll order room service, then," I said.

It wasn't quite how I'd envisioned our first family vacation without Dad, and it upset me to know that if he had been there, we would all have gone down to the fabulous restaurant and had a wonderful dinner together. Tammy wouldn't have dared keep the family waiting or run up a huge phone bill while she fought with her boyfriend, no matter how old she was!

"There's no need for you to do *that*," my mother huffed, as if I were fussing over nothing. "We'll go eat, Stacey."

We got dressed and headed to Palm Beach to enjoy a fancy meal and have some fun, even though most of our discussions were about Tammy and Garrett.

I felt stupid, like the problem was about food. But that was what we did as a family: we ate together. It was what all Jewish families did. In fact, there's a funny saying about Jewish holidays: "They tried to kill us. We won. Let's eat!" An old Jewish comedian, Jackie Mason, used to say that when you're in the theatre and the show's over, you can hear the Irish and Italian people asking, "Do you want a get a drink?" and you can hear the Jewish people asking, "Are you hungry? Wanna get something to eat?"

Unconditional Love

On previous vacations, we went out for breakfast and dinner, and no way Dad would ever wait to eat until 10! I felt out of sorts and confused. I felt *alone*. The fact nudged at the back of mind that, after my dad died, my family was changing as it continued to grow.

When we returned from Florida, Tammy broke off her engagement. I guess whatever the fight had been about had irreparably damaged their relationship, despite their attempts to salvage it during that lengthy phone call.

Mom said we had to go to Atlanta to help Tammy pack her stuff up and bring her back home to Philadelphia. She organized everything. Naturally, she never *asked* if we were available to go along with her plan—she just assumed we'd nod, agree, and drop everything, even though I'd recently given birth to my beautiful baby daughter Bari, to comply with whatever she wanted.

"We can all stay at Tammy's apartment," Mom said. "It'll be so much fun, all us girls together."

My heart sank. Sleep at Tammy's apartment? Would there be enough beds for all of us? Wait—weren't the movers taking all the furniture? I told Mom I was probably going to book a hotel room instead. She did *not* like that at all and told me so.

"Who are *you* to get a hotel room?" Mom snapped after a moment or two of deliberation.

"I'm a grown woman, Mom." I stood firm, determined not to allow her to bully me into submission. "And I *don't* want to sleep on the floor." Had Dad been there, nobody would have had to sleep on the floor, and we would be staying at the nicest hotel in Atlanta.

When we arrived, the movers greeted us at Tammy's apartment. They were just finishing up loading all the big furniture onto their truck, including the couch and beds. After they left, the four of us had nowhere to sit but on the floor, just as I'd feared.

As if things couldn't be any worse, my sister and her fiancé had previously bought a Rhodesian Ridgeback—a goliath of a dog who was big, boisterous, and *way* over-friendly. It also shed *everywhere*, and they expected to sleep on the floor among all the hair. I've never been a dog person, so this was a fresh hell for me.

"We can all stay up and talk," Mom announced as she walked around the emptied-out apartment. "It's going to be so much fun and great bonding time."

"I'm not sleeping on the floor, Mom." I surprised myself by standing up to her once. "It's uncomfortable and full of dog hair. That's why I got myself a hotel room. So, how about dinner?" I was in Atlanta for the first time and couldn't wait to experience the city and have a yummy meal.

However, my mom and sisters had another plan. "We're going to order salads for delivery," Mom said.

What?

Tammy told me the takeout place had the *best* salads, and she was so excited. Excited? Who on earth would want to be in Atlanta, sitting on the floor with all the dog hair, eating a salad?

Not me. But I had no choice.

That's what *they* wanted to do, and I once again went along with the plan. But I tell you what, I was *not* sleeping on that floor!

After dinner I prepared to go to my hotel and, for the first time in my life, I stood up to my mom. I was married and had enough money to book a room for one night. But all mom and my sisters wanted to do was sit on the floor of Tammy's desolate apartment and talk all night. There weren't even any snacks! Hahaha!

"You *have* to stay up all night with us." Lisa was becoming more insistent, likely at the behest of our mother. "It's not often we get time together these days, and who knows when the next time will be?"

"I'll stay 'til eleven, then I'm going to the hotel." It was already getting late, I was tired, and my ass was numb from sitting on the floor.

"That's way too early to go!" Tammy chimed in. "We're going to pull an all-nighter!" She appeared to be even more excited at the prospect than Mom. Perhaps my poor sister just needed the company since she was in the apartment she'd shared with the supposed love of her life until recently.

I could understand that.

"I know what we'll do!" Mom declared, getting to her feet. "I'll get a hotel room for *all* of us!"

I had that all too familiar sinking feeling in the pit of my stomach. I wanted to be alone!

"I can get a room with two double beds and have them put in a cot." Mom had obviously given her idea plenty of thought. "I don't mind taking the cot. And Stacey, you cancel your room."

I opened my mouth to argue but saw the determined look on her face. I knew from bitter experience she wasn't about to back down—it was either her way or she'd wear me down and make me feel like a terrible person in front of my sisters… and then I'd back down anyway. I thought it prudent to save myself the potential hours of Mom's guilt-tripping and cajoling, only for me to just give in to what she obviously thought was a reasonable compromise. I canceled my reservation and stayed in one hotel room with my mom and sisters. It was just like the "good old days."

Only, it wasn't. Not exactly.

I was beginning to see through the cracks a little more each day: the rules were changing. After Dad's passing, I began to question those Berger family traditions that had once made us so unique. For example, salad—*especially* takeout salad—had never, *ever* been an option when Dad was around. We'd always eat out at the very best restaurants wherever we were. There was no way on earth Dad would have allowed his family to sit on the floor in an empty apartment and eat salad!

Then, Mom started to date Mark. Mom was in love with him and became very serious about him very quickly. He whisked her away to New York City for a romantic weekend getaway, and I had chocolate-covered strawberries and champagne delivered to their hotel room. It was my way of letting Mom know I was happy she had found someone.

Sadly, she didn't appreciate my gesture. I was beginning to feel more and more like an outcast in my own family. I was trying to be myself, the way we always were as a family, but it just didn't feel the same. It felt like I was holding onto something that wasn't there anymore, and I didn't want to let go.

Things with Mom and my sisters only worsened. Tammy and Lisa were always on her side no matter what, and I wasn't getting along with them either. I was alone, sad, and confused.

I was also concerned about my dad's death. The doctor originally came out to tell us dad was going to be okay and then, an hour later, he had another heart attack and died. My concern was what happened during that hour? How long did it take for someone to get to him after this second heart attack? Was he neglected in any way? I wasn't angry with a desire to punish somebody. I just wanted to make sure that, if someone did make a mistake, I knew about it!

I planned to get Dad's records and have another cardiologist review them. And guess who I would send those records to? Dr. Nakhjavan I called Mom to let her know my intentions, and she didn't react favorably. In fact, she told me I couldn't retrieve dad's records. She said I needed to get over his death and move on. I explained how I was sure there was a statute of limitations and in a couple of years, we would no longer be able to access the documents. What if, in a decade or two, one of us wanted to review them? I just wanted to have them. She forbids me. Again, feeling alienated and misunderstood, I subpoenaed the records anyway and sent them to Dr. Nakhjavan. After he read them, he said nothing really could have been done to save my father, and I found peace with that. It would have bothered me if I hadn't asked him, for my own sake as well as Dad's.

Then Mom called to tell me, "I'm selling the condos in Atlantic City." She casually announced her decision as if it were nothing at all.

"All three of them?" I couldn't believe what I was hearing. Surely, she wasn't serious about letting *all* of our condos down the shore go. "Are you selling 1100?" That was the apartment we'd practically grown-up in. I had so many fond memories there.

"Yes," Mom said matter-of-factly. "I'm only keeping the third condo because it's already being rented." That was a good income for her.

"You can't do that, Mom."

"Mark is going to sell his house and, when I sell the condos, we'll buy a place on the beach together."

I was horrified. That condo was my second home! "You should keep the first one, at least, for the family," I told her.

"Who are *you* that you deserve your own condo?" Mom's words stung me even harder than the nasty, disapproving sound in her voice.

I called my sisters right away and, much to my dismay, they didn't care at all if my mom sold all the condos. They liked the idea of having a beach house with Mark and his family. Once again, I felt like an unwanted outsider in the family.

At that point, I didn't feel comfortable anymore around my mother. How could she not understand? I didn't think I *deserved* a condo, but I wanted to keep some memories of my dad alive. Was she really that oblivious to her own daughter's feelings? Or was she just trying to erase the past?

Chapter Thirty-Five:
The Letter

Nothing on earth hurts my soul deeper than conditional love.
—Brooke Bida

I grabbed the mail and found a letter with no postage stamp. It was my mom's handwriting. She had written me a letter, driven forty-five minutes to my house to put it in my mailbox, and left. The letter was so damaging and so painful that over the next twenty years, I completely forgot about it. The hurt was too much to bear. However, during Covid, while cleaning out the basement, I came upon that horrible letter.

It began with my mom telling me how *my dad has been dead for four and a half years* and claiming I'm *not handling it well.* She wrote *how terribly I have spoken to her* in the years since Dad passed away, how I have been *angry at her all that time*, and how I have *emotionally* and *verbally* abused her. She went on to explain how I am *jealous of my sisters' relationship with her.* And here was the big kicker for me: *You are having major problems with regard to your father's death.* As any loving and caring mom would, she decided to point out all my flaws and decides she doesn't want to have a relationship with me.

She then described how unhealthy my marriage was—at the time of her writing, I thought I was in a happy relationship, so it came across as her attacking the only good thing I thought I had left in this world. She was totally obsessed with the fact I smoked pot and added that *I escape the reality of my dad's death and unhappy marriage through my daily use of drugs.*

The *rage and anger* I displayed in our arguments was, according to Mom, out of control. She didn't mention the temper my father had my entire life. It was something I clearly got from him and something we all accepted when *he* lost *his* temper.

But it gets worse.

Mom writes: *You have lost all your old friends. You judge everyone negatively and fight with them about what they don't do for you... You have problems with your sisters and me.* Then, in all caps, *PLEASE stop smoking pot and get on medication for depression and anger management.*

I *was* on medication for anxiety and depression. My psychologist and psychiatrist both knew of my marijuana use, and I was on a specific medication that allowed for the use of recreational drugs. Mom's obsession with my pot use worsened to the point that she actually called the marriage counselor Jon and I were seeing. When I walked in for my next session, the therapist told me my mother had called her and told her I smoked pot *six times a day* and I needed emergency intervention. My therapist added that she had never received a call from an adult patient's parent unless it was a matter of life or death. My therapist rightly informed my mom that she could not discuss the matter with her.

Seeing my mom's controlling, over-dramatic behavior when I was a grown woman who was married with two kids, helped my therapist understand the problems in our relationship. In fact, Mom once came along with me to a session, and it was a total disaster! We left before our time was up because Mom couldn't see anything my way, and vice versa.

It was as if my mom imagined I was shooting up heroin and laying on the couch all day. When, in reality, my kids had great lunches packed, always made it to the bus on time, and I worked as a preschool teacher at my synagogue when my kids were in school full time, and I loved it. In fact, I loved it so much that I went back to college, Gratz College, to get my degree in early childhood education with an emphasis in Judaism. It was an ideal job for me. I worked Monday, Wednesday, and Friday until 3 p.m., and Tuesdays and Thursdays until 1 p.m. I could still get home for the kids after school and even had time to make dinner.

In the letter, my mom said she hoped I'd get off drugs. She said I *can go to therapy forever, but without the proper medication—which you cannot take until you stop smoking pot—you will not get better.* Had she become a doctor without telling me? I was on a medication that allowed me to smoke pot!

Without the benefit of a medical degree, Mom diagnosed me with a **mental illness**, which was even more painful to read. *If you had a physical illness, I would do all I could to get you the proper medical attention. This is a* mental *illness, Stacey.*

That was how my mom thought she was helping me handle my dad's death. She decided to break me down in every possible imaginary way she could: I had no friends, I was jealous of my sisters, *and* I had mental illness!

I can't talk to you anymore. She wrote, she'd reached her limit: no love, no caring, no nothing.

She continued, *If I didn't love you as much as I do, I wouldn't have taken the abuse from you for as long as I did in the hope that you would change.* She adds that she would *continue to love me regardless of how long it took me to get better,* putting the onus on me to return to her when I was healthier.

As a mom, I couldn't imagine ever trying to hurt my child in such a way, to punish them, to be so mean, and to break them down even more. How was Mom's behavior supposed to help me? Remember, it had been four years since Dad died, I had two toddlers and a failing marriage, and this was all the love and support my mom could find for me.

The letter was so painful I suppressed it and had forgotten about it until I found it during Covid while cleaning out the basement. I sat on the cold floor, crying and crying, each new line more painful than the one before. I couldn't believe my mom wrote these horrible things to me so soon after my dad died. That was the moment I decided to write this book.

Unconditional Love

Dear Stacey,

You've spoken to me last night the way you did for the very last time. You have been angry with me for over 4-1/2 years and you have verbally and emotionally abused me during that time. I cannot do more to show you that I love you. You are jealous of your sisters and their relationship with me. The reality of it is I spend more time with you than the two of them combined. No matter what I do, it isn't enough.

As far as you are concerned, I don't love you enough, I don't do enough for you, I don't spend enough time with you, and so on and so on. I see you and Josh and Bari every week because I want to; because I love you all, but it isn't good enough.

You are having major problems with regard to your father's death. You are escaping the reality of his death and your unhappy marriage through your daily use of drugs. You are ruining your life and your family's lives. Your abusive and aggressive behavior began well before your father died. His death only intensified it. Although you give your children a lot of love and affection, they are living in an environment that is filled with anger and dissension. Your aggressive behavior towards Jon – motivated by your unhappiness in your marriage, your grief over your father's death, and your own anger which goes back many years is not only frightening and sad for your children to see and live with, but will, in time, have a devastatingly negative psychological effect on their lives. It breaks my heart to have them witness all that is going on in their home.

The rage and anger that you displayed Tuesday towards Lisa was absolutely frightening. You literally behaved like a crazy person. Your anger is out of control. We talked all morning about the argument and I tried to support you and calm you down. I called you in the afternoon to see how you were doing and left a message that I hoped you were okay and I loved you, but that wasn't good enough for you. You attacked me with such hurtful accusations that were unjust and unwarranted and told me you'll just have to accept who I am, as though I have not been there for you and that I don't love you enough. This hurts me more than you can ever imagine.

This past week was more than I can take. You have taken me to my breaking point. I cannot be emotionally and verbally abused by you anymore. I have tried for 4-1/2 years to support you with your problems by coddling you, stroking you, being with you, telling and showing you how much I love you. It is not working any more. I don't deserve what you have been doing to me.

Take stock of your life. You have lost all of your old friends. You judge everyone negatively; fight with them about what they don't do for you. You have problems with the Waxman's and especially your sister-in-law Melissa. You have

Unconditional Love

problems with Jon, your sisters and me. You are alienating your family through your anger and negativity.

PLEASE stop smoking pot as excessively as you are, get on medication for depression and anger management and get your life back together again. Your children need and deserve a healthy mother.

If you had a physical illness, I would do all that I could to get you the proper medical attention. This is a mental illness and other than finding a therapist for you and trying to be there for you to guide you, support you and love you, I can't help you. I desperately want you to do all that you can to get better. Your sisters, husband, children and I all love you dearly and need you in our lives as the wonderful, sweet person you can be and were.

My only hope is that you will recognize what you are doing to yourself and your family and will want to get off the drugs so that you can think clearly and rationally. You can go through therapy forever, but without proper medication, which you cannot take until you stop smoking pot, you will not get better.

If I didn't love you as much as I do, I wouldn't have taken the abuse from you for as long as I did in the hope that you would change.

I love you with all my heart and regardless of how long this takes for you to get better, I will continue to love you.

Love Always and Forever,

Mommy

Chapter Thirty-Six:
He's in His Underwear

Around six months later, I visited a medium. I missed Dad so much and was desperate for any connection with him. My cousin Avi had told me of a medium in Baltimore, Maryland, who her mother-in-law said was incredible. I drove two hours to Baltimore to meet the woman and hopefully talk to Dad. I didn't know if I truly believed in ghosts, but I wanted to at least try.

The medium was an older woman and a Holocaust survivor. All she knew was my first name: I never filled out any paperwork, never gave her my address, and told her nothing about my family, my background, or any aspect of my life. Even if she discovered that information on her own—although we didn't have social media or anything like that back then—my last name was Waxman. Nothing would come up about the Berger family from that.

I walked in. She was nice, welcoming, and asked me to sit on one of the chairs in the middle of the room. We faced one another, knees touching, in an otherwise empty space. She smeared some kind of makeup, like concealer, onto my hand and "read" it.

She immediately stopped and looked up. "I have never done a reading before when a person is sitting here in his underwear," she declared with an embarrassed smile.

My heart skipped a beat!

Dad *always* sat around the house in his underwear, much to my mother's chagrin. He'd put on a robe if someone came, of course, but preferred to do everything around the house in his jockeys, tighty-whities. I couldn't believe that she said that! But the real zinger came when she told me about my mom and Mark. Mom was very in love with Marc, and they were planning their wedding.

"Your mother is not going to get married," she continued. "Her loved one is very sick in his stomach." She stopped for a second before adding that someone named Debbie was coming to take him away from Mom. Mark's first wife, who had died several years before, was named Donna. That was pretty darned close…

At that point in time, Mark was totally healthy. Because we weren't getting along, I couldn't go back home to my mom and sisters and say, "Hey, guess what? I went to a medium who said Mark was very sick, his deceased wife is taking him back, and you are not going to get married." I didn't think that would be received well at all, so I kept the information to myself.

You wouldn't believe that, just a month later, Mark was diagnosed with pancreatic cancer. Their wedding invitations were printed out, and they'd begun to organize the wedding. After Mark was diagnosed, they never mailed out the invitations.

It was a confusing and painful time in my life. I was separated from my family by their anger toward me, and I no longer felt welcome. Aunt Shirley called and told me how sick Mark was. She suggested I go see my mom. I was always able to talk to Aunt Shirley about my problems. I told her my mom wasn't even talking to me and described the mean letter she'd written to say she didn't want to have a relationship with me. Nonetheless, I listened to Aunt Shirley because I always wanted to do the right thing. I drove forty-five minutes downtown, parked on the city street, and walked to Mom and Mark's apartment building to spend time with them while Mark was sick, and I went every other evening. I always went alone; not even Jon offered to go with me. He never supported or protected me, be it from his family or mine.

I was so alone.

Heading up in the elevator to the apartment, I took deep breaths and made sure I was strong. When I entered the bedroom, I found Mark, Mom, and both my sisters sitting in the same bed, all in a straight line. It looked *so* weird. It reminded me of that scene with the grandparents in *Charlie and the Chocolate Factory*! My sisters had hired nannies to take care of their kids so they could be with my mom and Mark 24/7. I guess I seemed even worse to them because I hadn't done that, even though I had two toddlers and drove into the city every other night. But my family being my family, I felt like whatever I did just wasn't enough.

One visit, Mom, Mark, and my sisters made me feel so uncomfortable by not talking to me that I went into the kitchen and cleared out the pantry of all the old, expired food. She had stockpiled tons of it!

Another time, a Saturday afternoon, I again walked into the master bedroom to find Mom, Mark, Lisa, and Tammy all in the bed and, sitting at the bottom end and standing around, were some of Mark's family. The Flyers were in the playoffs, and a game was on. Playoff hockey—the best! I assumed we'd watch, but when I entered, the TV was off.

Oh no! What was I going to do?

I *needed* to see that game. It sounds crazy, I know, but no matter where we were, my dad would have prioritized the game—and we all would too. Sometimes, Mom and Tammy played Scrabble or read books in the background, but playoff hockey was *important* in the Berger family.

But now, nobody was watching it, and I was confused. I mustered up all my strength to ask if anyone would mind if I switched it on. Nobody really answered me, so I added, "I'll put it on mute. I must see it, though."

Mom's face turned sour. I knew I was standing on eggshells, even though it seemed like a harmless suggestion. Finally, mercifully, she let me turn on the TV and put the game on low. I felt like such a disruption to their space and was completely uncomfortable.

I was confused and hurt. Dad would have had it on, no matter what—no way he'd have missed the playoffs! Back in the mid- '70s, when Uncle Kenny became a rabbi, the Flyers had been in the playoffs, and the time of the game clashed with Uncle Kenny's indoctrination service. What did Dad do? He smuggled a mini-TV into the synagogue in a brown paper bag! This was back in the '70s—a mini-TV? It must have been very expensive, but at all costs, my dad was not going to miss the Flyers in the playoffs!

The funniest part of that story is my uncle wanted Dad to keep him up to date on the score throughout the service, so Dad sitting in the back of the sanctuary with his paper bag, holding up one finger on one hand and two fingers on the other indicate the score. By the end of the service, there were eight grown men huddled behind Dad, all staring into the bag and watching the game!

Another time we went to Williamsburg, Virginia for a family vacation. To dad's dismay, the Flyers were playing in the playoffs while we would be at Busch Gardens, Merchant's Square or taking a tour of colonial Williamsburg. This was going to be a problem. I remember my parents having a heated discussion about this and the result was: Dad staying in the hotel room to watch the game, while us girls went with Mom to do some eating and shopping.

Sadly, visiting my mom and Mark got even worse. I dropped by one time when Mark's son was at the house making dinner for everyone; it filled the house with the most delicious smells.

"I don't think there'll be enough food for you to stay for dinner, Stacey," Mom said bluntly.

I felt sick and in complete shock. I had never felt so unwanted and so hurt by my own mother. I wanted to say, "So I've just driven all the way down here, and you're telling me I can't stay for dinner? Are you kidding me? I wouldn't treat a stranger like this!" But I couldn't. I was too uncomfortable and scared to confront my mom.

Out of nowhere, my brother-in-law jumped in and said, "Of course there'll be enough."

But Mom's face told the rest of the story: I simply was not wanted there.

I hung around for another forty-five minutes and left before they had dinner.

Since I visited every alternate day, I called my mom two days later to let her know I'd be coming down that night. Who knew the worst was yet to come?

"You're not welcome to come here anymore," she said, her voice cold and emotionless. "Only people who love Mark and care about him are welcome here."

"Are my sisters allowed?"

"Of course. They love and care about Mark."

I couldn't believe what I was hearing. How could my own mother be so cruel and heartless to her own daughter?

Mark died shortly after that. Mom called to let me know about the funeral arrangements. Apparently, I wasn't welcome when Mark was alive, but I was expected to stand next to my mother at his funeral.

"You must sit in the limo with me, Stacey." She was back to her old self and dishing out orders. I knew her demand had nothing to do with wanting me there to support her in her grief. All she cared about was portraying the image of the "perfect family" she'd painstakingly maintained over the years. All that ever mattered to her was what other people thought.

"No, Mom." I stood up to her. "I'll be riding with my husband."

"No, Stacey." Mom was not about to back down. "You will be in *my* limo. And I want you to sit with me at the service and accept condolences."

It was the first time I'd stood up to my mother about something truly important and, while it made my heart pound hard in my chest, it was scary and exhilarating.

In the end, I rode to Mark's funeral in my own car and didn't sit beside Mom at the service. Nor did I accept condolences with her. I did sit behind her, though, and maybe that maintained the perfect family façade in her eyes.

Jon and I went back to the Shiva house and, after washing my hands as tradition dictated, I noticed the family photographs on the table in the middle of the entranceway. There were happy, smiling pictures of Mom, Mark, and of both of their families… my sisters, their husbands and their kids…

Only, there was none of me or my family, my kids.

Not one.

It was the ultimate—and final, as far as I was concerned—kick in the teeth.

Unconditional Love

It broke my heart to see the same old routine playing out as it had after Dad died—only it was me and my family, instead of my grandparents, who were the pariahs. No one dared talk to us for fear of incurring Mom's wrath. Dutiful as always, I ended up hanging out in the kitchen and cleaning up plates and glasses around the house. That kept me busy so I wouldn't have to sit around being ignored and feeling uncomfortable.

It was one of the most painful experiences of my life.

But the Berger family values were well and truly ingrained in me. I continued to respect my mother, despite her every effort to push me away. Sadly, that only provided her with more opportunities to be mean to me.

Chapter Thirty-Seven:
I am Punished

Family is supposed to be our safe haven. Very often, it's the place where we find the deepest heartache.

—Iyanla Vanzant

It was my tenth wedding anniversary. A year earlier, my husband and I planned a special vacation in Jamaica to mark the occasion and I'd asked Mom if she would take care of the kids while we were away. She'd told me, "Sure," and we left it at that.

Just a week before our vacation, she drove the forty-five minutes across town to our house to pop yet another letter into my mailbox. No visit, no knock on the door. She just left the letter and drove all the way back to the city again.

In this second letter, Mom said she was sorry, but *she wouldn't be taking care of the kids* while we were away, and that I had been *rude and disrespectful* to her for the last time!

"How could she do this to us?" Jon asked me, as if I knew the answer. My mom had become more of an enigma, more eccentric over the years after Dad passed, at least to me.

She couldn't come over and spend special time with her grandkids when I wasn't even going to be there? She was punishing me like I was a naughty child. She didn't even care about ruining our vacation. It was evil.

"I have no idea." It was all I could think of to tell him.

"Whatever it is, she's left us in a mess. We may have to cancel the vacation." Jon was annoyed.

The very idea devastated me. We had been looking forward to our tenth anniversary trip to Jamaica for a long time, and the thought of canceling so last minute was beyond upsetting. "We can't do that!" I was close to tears. As odd as Mom had been behaving, I couldn't believe she'd just leave us in the lurch like that.

"Well, we can't take the kids," Jon replied.

"There must be something we can do!" I was desperate. I knew we couldn't ask Jon's parents because they'd made it very clear early in our marriage that they refused to babysit for any longer than a day every now and then.

Luckily, as I was crying and in shock after reading Mom's letter, Jon called our babysitter and asked if she could come for the week and look after the kids. Thankfully, she said yes, so we could still go!

But Mom had wanted me to lose all that money and not be able to travel for my anniversary. Who would do that? Even though I was happy we avoided my mom's punishment, I was deeply upset about the way she was treating me.

Chapter Thirty-Eight:
Our Jamaican Adventure

By coincidence, our next-door neighbors Michelle and David had connections with someone in Jamaica who owned a lot of businesses and property. Upon hearing Jon and I were vacationing there, they told us if we ever got into trouble or needed anything at all, we should ask for the Rollinses and drop their names.

At the time, I shrugged their offer off as just one of those nice things neighbors and friends say to one another, but little did I know just how handy it would come in.

We arrived early in the morning at the Ritz Carlton Hotel in Montego Bay, fresh from the plane and ready to start our vacation in earnest. It had been a stressful few years, not helped one bit by my mother and her last-minute snub, and I was more than ready to reconnect with my husband and relax together. We'd stayed at the hotel at least five times before and had booked the room we wanted well in advance. What we didn't know, of course, was that the Rollins family owned the very land upon which the Ritz Carlton stood.

"I'm sorry, but your room is not ready yet," the sweet, young receptionist told us with a warm smile. We'd left on an early flight from Philadelphia and arrived in Jamaica around noon. The receptionist told us to get some lunch and come back afterward to check.

It was still early, so we figured housekeeping hadn't gotten around to preparing our room yet. "Let's leave our luggage here and go eat," I said to Jon, and off we went.

Unconditional Love

We returned to the reception desk an hour or so later—plenty of time for them to have our room cleaned and ready for us.

"I'm sorry, Mr. and Mrs. Waxman," the pretty receptionist greeted before we had time to speak. "Your room isn't ready. In fact, the room you wanted is not available. But we do have Room 376 ready. I can have the busboy take up your luggage."

"That's not the room we booked." I kept my voice as calm as I could manage, just like my dad would.

The hotel was shaped like a U, with oceanfront rooms at both tops of the U. We knew from experience the rooms on the left side of the U were above a restaurant and caught the exhaust from the kitchens down on the ground floor, which filled them with a whole manner of food smells that could be quite unpleasant! We had specifically asked for our room to be on the right side of the U, which was precisely why we had booked that room a year before!

I thought back to how Dad would handle such a situation. With grace, charm, and money in the right hands!

Jon didn't do any of the talking. In fact, I didn't feel like he was supporting me at all. I think he thought I was being a complete bitch by demanding we get the right room, the one we'd booked.

"I'd like to speak with the manager." I fought to remain calm. I was prepared to grease a few palms if necessary. Dad would have been proud of me.

"It would be my pleasure," said the receptionist. *Her pleasure?* That was what they *had* to say at the Ritz Carlton, although it seemed so sarcastic.

"I'm so sorry, Mrs. Waxman." The manager, a tall, smartly dressed guy with a strong accent, did look genuinely apologetic. "We won't be able to give you the room you booked, but I can assure you the room you have is just as beautiful."

That was not acceptable to me at all. The rooms on the left, despite their different locations and the smells emanating from the restaurant below, cost the same amount of money as the ones to the right. We didn't want to stay on the opposite side of the hotel, spending a fortune on an expensive suite we couldn't fully enjoy.

I decided to drop the name my neighbors had given me. Of course, I had no idea if the manager would even know who they were. "If we had any problems, we were told to ask for Mrs. Rollins." I looked him square in the eye as I spoke, my stance unwavering.

At that, everything changed. And I do mean *everything*.

"How do you know Mrs. Rollins?" The manager was skeptical, unsure if I really knew her.

I replied that our neighbors are good friends with her and had told us to ask for her by name if we needed anything.

Unconditional Love

At that, the manager sent us back to the beach or pool or wherever we wanted to go, still without our room. He gave us keys to another room so we could change or shower if we wanted to. He had our bags taken to that room. "Come back in a couple hours." He turned on his heel and hurried away.

We went to the beach. Still wearing the clothes we'd traveled in, I read my book and Jon slept in his chair. After a while, we left and went to the room they had given us to tide us over while we waited. As soon as we walked in, I saw the little red light flashing on the telephone, meaning we had a message. Thinking it was reception letting us know our booked room was ready for us, I picked up the receiver and pushed the button.

"This is Mrs. Rollins's bodyguard and chauffeur," a deep, booming voice greeted me. "Mrs. Rollins would like to invite you for dinner tonight." There was a definite *something* in the guy's tone that told me it wasn't a request. He continued, "I am waiting in the lobby for you."

I panicked. I was still wearing the same sweat suit from early that morning! I didn't want to go, but Jon said we had to. And he was right—it wasn't optional. I changed the tank top under my sweat suit to something a little more fashionable, and Jon threw on jeans and a t-shirt. We expected to meet Mrs. Rollins at one of the seven restaurants on the hotel's property, so figured our attire was appropriate. We got ready in double time and made our way down to the lobby, planning to ask at the front desk who this bodyguard-chauffeur was if we couldn't find him ourselves.

But right away, we found him waiting for us. He smiled and instructed us to get in his car to go meet Mrs. Rollins.

Get in his car?

What?

Jamaica was not an entirely safe place, and tourists were told to never leave the hotel property! Nevertheless, we got into the car and went for a ride. I was scared to know where we were going, especially as we climbed higher and higher into the mountains. After twenty minutes or so, we pulled up to a fabulous, gated home set well away from any other dwellings, not a single neighbor to be seen.

At the gates stood a pair of burly armed bodyguards who looked far from welcoming holding huge rifles. That was the first time I'd seen an AK-47 outside of a movie! Beyond the imposing iron fence, the massive Rollins home nestled in a sweeping compound, with two roads heading in opposite directions. Our car came from the right and pulled up in front of Mrs. Rollins's house. The entrance was complete with an indoor decorative pool.

A butler greeted Jon and me at the door. He escorted us to the patio at the rear of the house. There was *another* pool back there—this one for swimming.

Michelle Rollins, the lady of the house, was having a small dinner party. I counted eight guests, including Jon and me.

"Are *you* the Waxman's?" She met us with an outstretched hand and a warm grin. "I was expecting someone much older." That figured. She likely thought a Jewish couple complaining to the manager at the Ritz Carlton would be in their sixties at the very least!

It was a spectacular evening. Mrs. Rollins—she insisted we call her Michelle—was most welcoming, and the rum drinks flowed endlessly. We learned she owned the local rum plantation and distillery, as well as pretty much everything else in the vicinity, and had a constant supply of real 80 proof Jamaican rum. I hated the taste but continued to drink the stuff out of respect for our hostess.

Our fellow party guests comprised three rich single women from Delaware Dupont Country Club, a single male real estate developer, and a gay couple. It was quite a cozy soiree.

The butler summoned us to dinner and, upon arriving at the table, Michelle separated Jon and me. She wanted my husband to sit next to her. Although I trusted Jon implicitly around other women (which ended up being a joke, as I soon discovered), I couldn't help but be a little upset because I didn't want to sit on the other side of the table with people I didn't know. I wanted to sit next to my husband.

Michelle was a good twenty years older than us. I guessed she was in her mid-fifties. She had weathered exceptionally well and had been Miss Delaware in the Miss America pageant back in the day.

The dark wood table was huge and square, set with exquisite silverware. An army of servants delivered our food covered with large silver domes. They waited until each plate was in place before lifting the cloches in perfect sync. It was quite theatrical! The meal, all fresh, local Jamaican fish and vegetables, was beyond delicious, and washed down with copious amounts of authentic Jamaican rum. The alcohol tasted to me a lot like gasoline—I guess I just wasn't used to it—and it was far too easy to get wasted on the stuff. Thankfully, I was not the only one becoming increasingly intoxicated as dinner went on.

Even the dessert was laced with rum! It was a beautifully homemade rum-raisin ice cream… with yet *more* rum poured over it. *Yuck!* I faced down this huge bowl of vanilla ice cream—I'm a chocolate lover and hate vanilla—with raisins (ew!) and rum poured straight out of the bottle on top. The guy next to me *ooh*ed and *ahh*ed at how delicious it was, and I was mixing my spoon through it, playing with it like a five-year-old who didn't want to eat her vegetables.

After dinner, Michelle caught up with us as we made our way with the other guests back to the patio. "I'd like to see you in my office," she said.

Not sure what to expect, we followed, only to discover Michelle Rollins's office was her bedroom.

"I'm not sleeping with her for a good room at the hotel!" I hissed at Jon.

"Tell me." Michelle sat at an antique desk near the edge of her expansive bed. "What is wrong at the hotel?"

We both felt bad saying anything negative to Michelle after having such a fabulous dinner at her home with her friends. But she insisted, so we told her about the whole ordeal we'd been through early that afternoon and the fact we still didn't have a room.

Michelle said she would take care of it, and we didn't need to worry. "When you go back to the hotel, you will have a new room with your key. Ask for it at the front desk when you return."

We did as instructed. The moment the chauffeur dropped us back off at the Ritz Carlton, we went straight to the front desk. Our room was immediately upgraded from the one we wanted to the Presidential Suite! Jon and I had gone from being the biggest losers to having the best suite in the place. We both felt like royalty!

We bumped into Michelle Rollins and her party guests throughout our vacation, and it was nice to make a few friends. We couldn't help but call Jon's parents to share the news of our exciting, crazy night, and they were ecstatic for us!

But the whole thing came with a tinge of regret for me: I couldn't call my own mother and tell her after she had just refused to watch my kids.

Chapter Thirty-Nine:
Insanity

> *Doing the same thing over and over and expecting different results.*
>
> —Merriam-Webster, "Definition of Insanity"

I spent the next twenty years trying to figure out a way to get along with my mom and sisters. When my sister got married, none of them were talking to me. I went to a therapist for some advice or mental tools I could use to get through the wedding, and his advice was to skip it. But I told him I *had* to go—it was my sister! The therapist said if things were *that* bad between us, I *really* shouldn't go.

Well, unfortunately, that wasn't an option for me.

What made matters worse was when my other sister got married and I received my bridesmaids dress in the mail in a bag. I wasn't as thin as either of my sisters, and I didn't look good in everything I tried on. I was very selective about what styles I wore, that I felt most comfortable in. In the bag was a high neck sleeveless dress that went all the way down to the floor. High necklines made my big boobs look like they went from my neck to my waist. It was the worst style for me, and I never wore it. In addition, I hated my arms and avoided sleeveless tops. I preferred an off-the-shoulder look because it covered part of my arms.

The dress was horrible. I was the bride's sister, a grown woman and a mother, and nobody even cared if I was going to be comfortable in the outfit. I could have used the exact same fabric to make a style that would complement me, and I would have felt good in. But I wasn't allowed, and even asking was rude.

Chapter Forty:
Divorce

> *Divorce is expensive. I used to joke they were going to call it "all the money," but they changed it to "alimony." It's ripping your heart out through your wallet.*
>
> —Robin Williams

In September 2009, I filed for divorce.

In the spring of that year, things between my husband and me had drastically changed. We didn't communicate the way we always had, and it felt to me like we were just... *off*.

We hired a babysitter every Saturday night so we could go out to drink and party with friends. We never went out alone; it was always with other people. Looking back, I realize Jon never wanted to be alone with me. We'd go to the fanciest, most upscale, place-to-be-seen restaurants. I begged him to go to Friendly's instead, get high, order grilled cheese and milkshakes, and stay in sweatpants, not to get all dressed up. Just to be together. But that was never an option.

Even when the Eagles were playing Monday night football, Jon watched at his friend's, where girlfriends or wives weren't included. I requested he watch just the first half with me, but he always said no. I sat and watched the games by myself.

We went to marriage counseling, but it seemed to not work at all. In the spring of 2009, I started to recognize that Jon was different. When we argued, it wasn't

Unconditional Love

the same way we argued before. He simply didn't care at all about me or anything I had to say. When we went out on Saturday night, he was more than mean to me. It was something I had never experienced from him before. But I still thought that we belonged together, and this was just a setback that we would fix.

One Friday night, I volunteered at my synagogue to help serve Shabbat dinner for an event. As I cooked in the kitchen, Jon took Bari to the playground behind the synagogue. Apparently, Marla showed up. She was my friend, but she was closer to my sister-in-law, Jon's sister, Melissa. Later that night, Bari came to me, eight years old, and told me she thought "Daddy likes Marla."

What?

I couldn't believe what I was hearing. But then again, things had been bad between Jon and me.

Bari continued that Marla came to the park and went to the jungle gym. She told Daddy to catch her if she fell. She indeed let go, and Daddy caught her. "I think Daddy likes her."

Wow!

I confronted Jon and relayed what our daughter had said.

Don't forget I'd been with him since I was twenty-two and married him at twenty-four. I thought he was my soulmate. I thought we belonged together. Little did I know how horrible my marriage really was, and it seemed everyone around us could see it but me.

I justified to myself the way Jon treated me as; *you can't have everything*. I had a beautiful life and accepted his rudeness as a price to pay. I told myself I had so much love from my parents and sisters that it made up for the love I didn't receive from my husband.

However, after my dad died, he refused to do anything to help Mom, which worsened things between my family and me. I felt like I had to choose between them and I, of course, picked my husband. But Jon didn't support me, and I was left alone to deal with the loss of my family.

And then I had to deal with the loss of my husband.

When I confronted Jon about what Bari told me, he said I was crazy and blew me off.

Another time, Jon took the kids out for ice cream, and guess who showed up? Yup.

Marla.

Josh came right home and said he had to tell me something, but he didn't want me to get upset. He described how Daddy gave Marla his jacket because she'd been cold. He said he thought Daddy liked Marla.

Again, I confronted Jon—this time with what Josh had told me.

Again, my husband told me I was crazy.

Unconditional Love

In May, on Mother's Day, we all went over to my sister-in-law's house for a barbeque. Things were particularly uncomfortable between Jon and me, but the kids would leave for camp a month later. I thought we could figure things out then.

We walked into my sister-in-law's kitchen, and guess who was there?

Marla!

It turned out Marla wasn't getting along with her husband and had asked if she could spend Mother's Day with the Waxman's. I looked over to see her cuddling with Bari and tickling my daughter's arm. I got a weird, shrinking feeling in my stomach, but I immediately ignored it.

The next weekend, my kids wanted to go to movie night at Talamore, the pool we belonged to. Jon and I were going out, as we did every Saturday night, so I called my sister-in-law to ask if she could pick Bari and Josh up after the movie. She couldn't, but said Marla was there and she'd offered to pick them up for me. I thought that was so nice of her.

Little did I know, or *refuse* to see, that Marla was slowly creeping her way into my family.

The next Friday, Marla came over to our house to bring me a challah for Shabbat. Again, *so* nice.

At the end of June, my kids got on the bus to leave for overnight camp. Jon and I went out for breakfast and headed over to the Talamore pool. After a day at the pool, we went to Pumpernicks, the best Jewish deli in Philly, for an early dinner.

When we got home, Jon calmly told me he wanted a divorce. And that was the beginning of my second worst nightmare. I didn't want my kids to be part of a divorced family.

In all, it took us six years to get divorced. Our business was all cash, and it was difficult to show how much money Jon made. All his filing cabinets were in our basement, which was also where he worked on his bills and paperwork. Three days after finding out Jon wanted a divorce, I took every paper in the filing cabinets to Staples and made copies of *everything*. A couple months later, Jon told me I could look at his documents in the file cabinet. I informed him that I'd already copied them all.

Every Monday night after we separated, Jon came back to the house and retreated into the basement to do his paperwork. One time, he walked in after I had just served the kids dinner. Out of respect, while the kids were sitting at the table eating, I asked Jon if he wanted some food as well. Politely, he said no. I left to give him time alone with the kids. Josh told me later that, as soon as I'd gone, Daddy had said, "Give me that chicken." Ha!

What was not so funny was that after he was done in the basement, Jon would leave papers ripped up in the trash can. Ripped up? So, someone wouldn't see them? Well, *I* was going to see them! Every Monday night, I went down after he'd left and taped the shreds back together. They contained the *real* numbers for our business and would benefit me greatly later when trying to prove his income.

From day one, Jon treated me like *I* was the cheater. He was painfully mean to me throughout. It was so confusing. I honestly wouldn't treat a stranger the way my own husband treated me. I was the mother of his children, and he showed absolutely no respect for me. What a terrible example for my kids to see. It was not the way a man should ever act toward a woman. It wasn't the way anyone should treat anybody! Such anger! But I didn't cheat! He did!

The next summer, when the kids left for camp, we all went out for breakfast as a family. When the check came, Jon made me pay for my scrambled eggs! $5. It was humiliating. That was just the beginning of him regarding me like a piece of shit. Every time he made me fork over money when we went out as a family— he even made me pay for half of the kids' food—it broke me down. Eventually, though, I began to expect it and accept it. But it was still so upsetting for me.

My mom assisted me with legal and accounting fees. She helped me pay real estate taxes, overnight camp, and for Bari's bat mitzvah. I was so thankful and appreciated all she did for me and my kids.

Every summer, Jon would refuse to pay for our kid's overnight camp. He expected my mom to pay; she had enough money. The day before the first day of camp, I would get a call that my kids will not be allowed on the bus unless our bill is paid. It would be a contest to see who would cave in first and pay – Jon or my mom. My mom told the kids that they shouldn't worry because she would make sure they went to camp. My mom strongly held out to the very last second when Jon was forced to pay for his own kids. He always paid for them to both go to overnight camp before the divorce, so these summers should be no different.

For Bari's bat-mitzvah, he told me that if I didn't help pay for the caterer, that my guest would not be able to get alcoholic drinks. Furthermore, he told me that his guests would have wrist bands to show they can order alcohol. No center pieces on my tables unless I paid for them. Even told the photographer not to take pictures of me and my family since I couldn't pay for that either. I had none of my own money. My mom refused to have wrist bands at her granddaughter's bat mitzvah and paid for whatever was needed.

That's just a taste of what I went through. Now, I don't intend for this book to be about my divorce—that's a whole other book by itself! One day, I'll write about my dating experiences, which will make a crazy read! But that's all for another day.

Chapter Forty-One:
Alone

On top of my dad dying and my disconnection from my mom and my sisters, my husband was leaving me. So much loss. So much abandonment. So much pain.

But I was always okay. I always kept going.

For the first time in my life, I was alone. I went from being part of a family in which I was *never* alone, an enmeshed family I needed therapy to understand, to being completely by myself.

Unfortunately, my sheltered upbringing left me wholly unprepared for the outside world. Would you believe I didn't even know how to pump gas when I got divorced at the age of forty-two?

Not only was I on my own, but I had to start supporting myself, and that was something I'd also never had to do before. I'd gone from having my dad take care of me to having my husband take care of me.

Throughout my life, I'd never paid for my own car or car insurance or for my clothes or spending money or a mortgage or any bills—my parents paid for all of it. No school loans. When I went to law school, I lived in my own townhouse, fully furnished and paid for by my parents. Then I got married, and my husband took care of me. And then, when I got divorced and was faced with having to do everything for myself—including paying bills and pumping my own gas—it all came as one heck of a shock!

I got a second job. While I taught preschool during the day, I started to teach in the Hebrew High School at night and on the weekend. I taught seventh grade

Unconditional Love

Jewish Studies and loved it. I was the coolest religious schoolteacher, and I really wanted to share my love of Judaism and our culture and traditions.

Part of my curriculum involved teaching about the Holocaust. In my class, I'd talk about other kids, the same as my own students, who were told one day at school that all the Jewish kids had to go sit at a different table for lunch. How the Nazi soldiers would go into the homes of Jewish families with kids their age, who would have to hide in closets or under the floors. We discussed friends they had who weren't Jewish, and asked if *their* families would hide them from the Nazis. There were really no answers to these questions. But the Jewish people, regarding the Holocaust, say, "Never forget." I raised my own kids to be proud to be Jewish.

It's interesting to me that Jewish people never really fight back. We just take it on the chin and move on. Even when I used to get thrown into the lockers at school by the bullies, my parents never did anything, and I went back to school every day. It was the same with my own kids; I didn't go into school or call the bullies' parents to confront them about their antisemitism. I simply repeated my parents' behavior and told my children to take it and be proud to be Jewish.

So, I had two jobs and was now a single mom with two kids. I worked at the preschool during the day and the Hebrew High School two nights a week and on Sundays. But it didn't last long: I could not support myself on a preschool teacher's salary.

I was a lawyer. I had a law degree, but hadn't practiced in over twenty years, which meant my license was retired. I had to get it reinstated, and that consisted of taking many hours of CLE, Continuing Legal Education, courses and applying to the Courts to renew my license to practice law.

I completed the process and was able to get a job as a staff attorney for an excellent securities litigation firm, where I stayed for the next eight years until I was laid off during the Covid pandemic. My old first boyfriend from high school was an attorney at this firm, the senior partner was somebody I'd gone on a date with in college who I wasn't interested in at that time (big mistake, ha!), another one of my senior partners had come to my house in high school when I had a party, and another one of the senior partner's sons was good friends with my daughter from camp. It was humbling to be a staff attorney, the lowest on the totem pole, and work for these men. But I was so thankful to have a job and worked as hard as I could.

***

During this time, my cousin Ilana got married. I went to the wedding. I felt a little uncomfortable because of all the tension in our family. Sitting at my table, I look at the dance floor to see Uncle Sammy, Aunt Tris, Ilana and her new husband

Unconditional Love

Danny all together, smiling and celebrating. I could feel the happiness and love they shared. But I was so confused: wasn't Uncle Sammy the bad one in the family? Hadn't he let my parents down? Well, it certainly didn't look that way to me. It looked like my parents let my cousin down while Uncle Sammy and Aunt Tris had provided her with a loving family. Later, I wrote a letter to my aunt and uncle, feeling the need to share my emotions with them about how beautiful the wedding had been and how much love and happiness they had given to Ilana.

Now, twenty years later, Ilana is so close with Uncle Sammy and Aunt Tris, and they are a strong, blissful family. While my family had once been the stalwart one, we were now broken. Not even broken—gone. I admire Uncle Sammy and the family he created for my cousins.

Chapter Forty-Two:
A Vacation With Mom

Enmeshment –…intrusive demands for support or attention…
—Melissa Saunders

Mom decided, fifteen years after Dad passed away, to take all of us on a vacation to Jamaica for her birthday. This vacation, for me, was a nightmare, and I ended up with over half a dozen cold sores on my lip! The vacation crowd comprised of my sisters and their husbands and kids, Mom, and me and my kids. I was already divorced by that time. My sisters' kids were young, around five- to ten-years-old. My kids were around sixteen or seventeen.

The resort had a big pool for teenagers and parents and, in another area, one for kids, which had a cool water slide. Josh, Bari, and I went to the teenage pool, while everyone else sat at the children's area. I was happy, my kids were happy, and I was sure my sisters' kids were having a great time on that awesome kiddie water slide.

Apparently, though, not everyone was content: I received a visit from my sisters, who told me I should be sitting with Mom and them. They explained that Mommy had taken us all on the trip, so I should spend time with her and the rest of the family.

My kids were almost adults and didn't want to be around the youngsters, and I certainly didn't either. Tons of noisy little kids ran around, and the chairs were all crammed together. Also, there was a drinking and swimming contest coming up at the teenage pool that my kids were excited to participate in. Plus, I was meeting parents who had children the same age as mine. It was a completely different atmosphere than at the kiddie pool.

I told my sisters I would visit with them shortly and that we had breakfast, lunch, and dinner together, that my kids wanted to hang out with other teens, and I wanted to meet more adults my own age. My sisters insisted, but I stayed where I was with Josh and Bari.

I think that was when my first stress-induced cold sore popped up, the first of an entire family of cold sores that would take their own vacation on my lip for the entire trip in Jamaica.

My family was also upset that my kids consumed alcohol. Given the drinking age in Jamaica was eighteen, I was fine with them having fun together. Nonetheless, I was forced to listen to comments from my mom and sisters about *my* children's drinking. All I could do was ignore them. All the kids Josh and Bari hung out with were their age, and they were enjoying alcoholic beverages too!

Chapter Forty-Three:
Painful Parties

> *A dysfunctional family is not a family at all, it's a toxic relationship parading as a requirement.*
>
> —Michelle Meleen

As the years went by, my sisters seemed so concerned about my kids' alcohol consumption that one of them called me before their daughter's bat mitzvah and asked me to make sure they didn't drink too much at the party. What? Josh was already twenty-one, and I couldn't control what he did! It was ridiculous! They were supposed to go to those parties and have fun with their cousins.

I once went to my sister's birthday party, and one of her friends asked who I was. I told her I was the party girl's sister. The woman looked at me and said, "Wow, you *really* are a black sheep!" She turned out to be one of my sister's best friends.

At another party for that same sister, I was talking outside with some of her friends (and probably smoking a joint) when another group walked by. Someone's husband declared out loud, "Look, the black sheep is here!"

I always felt so uncomfortable at those parties. I really wish I'd not felt so obliged to attend.

At my other sister's Halloween party, one of her friends came up to me and said, "I didn't even know she had another sister."

Unconditional Love

That was the last of her parties I attended. Around 11 p.m., I prepared to drive back to Philly. I'd been there since eight that evening and was dressed in costume like everybody else. It was a '70s theme, and guess what I went as? Yup, a bag of weed! I'd found a t-shirt that was made to look like a baggie, I wore a marijuana hat, green eyeshadow, and green lipstick. I went to say goodbye to my mom, and she told me I couldn't leave yet because my sister hadn't served dessert. I obeyed Mom as I always did and continued walking around in circles by myself. Twenty minutes later, my sister still hadn't served dessert, and I *really* wanted to go home. I went to kiss my mom goodbye again, and she repeated that I couldn't leave until we had dessert. At that point, I'd had enough. I grabbed my jacket and my pocketbook, walked to my car, and left. Did I *really* need my mom's permission to go home at almost fifty years old?

And this uncomfortable, isolated feeling also applied to my nieces' and nephew's birthday parties. I was never introduced to any of their friends, and my mom and sisters ignored me. At one such gathering, my sisters gifted me a Pandora bracelet for my birthday. Their good friend who sold the bracelets, whom they'd bought mine from, was also in attendance. I already had one of the charms they gave me, so I approached the woman and told her I wanted to exchange it. She told me, quite bluntly, that I couldn't.

In shock at her reaction, I said, "I'll pay extra if I need to, but I already have this charm and would like to get a different one."

Very coldly, she again said, "Sorry, you can't."

I felt so uncomfortable I went inside my sister's house and sat in one of the bedrooms by myself and cried. In the end, I decided to leave the bracelet on the island in the kitchen, got in my car, and prepared for my two-hour ride back to Philadelphia. That was the last kids' birthday party I went to.

I summoned up the courage to confront my sisters about how they never talked to me at their kid's birthday parties. Lisa said she was always so busy with all the guests that she never found a chance. Tammy said I alienated myself. But they never once approached me to have a conversation or try to understand my perspective. Whenever I tried to describe how I felt, like I didn't belong in our family, it would end up in a fight because they defended themselves and my mom to the end.

For years, I found the only way to get along with my mom and sisters was to be fake—not show my true feelings, add no real comments to our conversations, and just go with their flow. I was still the outcast and, instead of trying to include me, they said I alienated myself.

Mom insisted I go to therapy. She'd picked the therapist and said she'd pay for it. When the therapist started comparing my mom and sisters to the Stepford wives, Mom changed her mind and refused to pay.

Unconditional Love

I also saw a psychiatrist who explained things so clearly. He said my mom and sisters were like a gang. You had to be *in* the gang, or you were out. You couldn't just show up for holidays and birthdays. You couldn't just have one foot in. It was all or nothing. I was not in their gang anymore, nor did I want to be.

Chapter Forty-four:
Avi and The Needlemans

One of the best trips I ever took was for my fiftieth birthday. I asked both my sisters and my cousin, Avi to celebrate with me. We were all in agreement to go on a cruise until the cabin arrangements were suggested. Avi and I had already discussed that we each wanted our own room with a balcony and would try to book rooms next to or near each other. My sisters, on the other hand, wanted all four of us to be in one cabin. What? This wasn't spring break. We are not in college. We were grown women.

Since we couldn't agree and I was *not* going to share a room with them, we looked for other options. The Rolling Stones had just announced a new European tour and were going to play in Amsterdam. That was what I wanted to do: go to Amsterdam—I had never been before—and see the Rolling Stones in concert. Avi and I shared the same love for the Stones, but my sisters did not so much. But they had never seen the Stones perform, and it would've been so amazing for us all to share an experience like that. My sisters said they couldn't go because they were afraid to leave the country with all the terrorist attacks. That didn't stop us. Avi and I traveled to Amsterdam, and we had *the best* time. We got seats in the pit, four rows from the stage. We got up every morning, sat on the water canal, had coffee, and smoked pot we bought from the Bulldog Café. We flew in Thursday night and flew back Monday morning. What an adventure!

During the same weekend Avi and I went to Amsterdam, a mass shooting occurred at the MGM Grand in Las Vegas during a music festival. Can you imagine if I'd changed my trip to Vegas, so my sisters didn't have to leave the country, only to experience a terrorist attack right here in the US?

Avi became one of my best friends, and over the years, we've grown close as sisters.

Over the years, Avi and I developed a very special friendship. When my sister got married, she held her bachelorette party in Philly. Avi came in for the big night, and we decided to stay together at the Ritz Carlton, right around the corner from the venue. I told my sisters to stay with us, but they didn't want to. Before the party, Avi and I got our hair done. As we walked back and up the steps to the Ritz Carlton, we both stopped for a second and said we hoped our dads could see us together. We woke up in the morning and ordered eggs benedict from room service. We always wanted to do the same things, and I was more like her than I was my own sisters.

When Avi got married, we all flew to Jamaica for her bachelorette party. It was so much fun. Neither of my sisters could make it.

Even when my cousin Ricky got married, I was a bridesmaid at his wedding. My sisters weren't. I always seemed to be separated and making different decisions than them.

As we got older, Avi had a family of her own. When she went on vacation with her husband or on a quick trip to see the Rolling Stones in concert somewhere, I would drive from Philly to Baltimore to stay at her house and take care of her kids, twin boys and daughter. At the boys' bar mitzvah, she seated me at her table with her family and closest friends. I didn't sit with my mom and my sisters. My mom asked me why I wasn't sitting with them. I just looked at her and made a face that suggested- I don't know. Avi and her husband Gabe always made me feel special and wanted.

I also treasure the relationship I have with Avi's kids and wish I had a similar one with my own nieces and nephew. Avi and I have gone on vacation with our kids together. Over Covid, Avi, her daughter, and I went to Miami and stayed at the Ritz Carlton in South Beach for two nights and then stayed at my son's apartment in Brickel for two nights, while he was a way on vacation. Another time her family was going to Jamaica over Thanksgiving and asked me to go with them. I got my own room and was on my way.

When Avi had surgery on her shoulder, I was already living in Miami, and she flew all three kids to me to watch while she recovered. I loved every minute of it!

Her boys are now in college in Tampa and, when they come to Boca or Miami, they always call me and ask if we can meet for dinner or if they can come over and see me for a little. One time, they even brought their college roommates with them. I love being so close to them and enjoy all the time we spend together.

Unconditional Love

And, because Avi is Switzerland, I respect her relationships with my mom and my sisters and never suggest she shouldn't be close with them because of how they treat me. That is the one thing I do not want to repeat from my parents.

However, when my sisters took their kids to college, they used Avi as a go-between, knowing she would call me and tell me what they were saying about me. They relayed to Avi how hurt and upset they were that I hadn't called them or their children, when they were headed to college for their freshman year. My first reaction was wondering, *how am I supposed to know the exact day they left when nobody is talking to me?* Of course, I then called my sisters to discuss what they had said to Avi about me. My sisters started another fight with me and proceeded to tell me I *"ruined one of the most important days in their lives"* by not phoning them on the day they left with the kids for their first year at Penn State. They wouldn't leave me alone or stop attacking me.

They acted as if I completely ignored my niece and nephew going to college. In fact, when they both graduated from high school, my gift was a new TV for their dorm room. I wanted to get them a nice smart TV that would hook up to their computer. Well, that was a problem too. My sister told me I was spending too much money, which was none of her business. Then she told me she called Penn State and learned they didn't have cable access, so they couldn't have TVs in the dorms. What? I called the school and talked to someone in the housing department and explained my situation. The lady I spoke with, by coincidence, had sisters who weren't very nice to her, and she said that was the most ridiculous thing she'd ever heard! All the kids had TVs in their dorm rooms. I ended up sending each kid a check for $250 to get an awesome TV for college. I have no idea what they did with the money.

Chapter Forty-Five:
Never Good Enough

It was heartbreaking when my sister's annual mammogram showed breast cancer. It was so upsetting. She decided to have a double mastectomy. I sent her a t-shirt with *under construction* written across the chest. I ordered personalized stationery with her name, that had golf and martini images with the pink breast cancer ribbon. I baked my famous cake pops with all pink decorations. I worked full time and tried to text her every day to see how she was doing. She ended up telling me that texting was "not making an effort" to be there for her. Pushing me away again. Whatever I did was never good enough. I attended a breast cancer walk to support her. We gathered, all her friends and family. I spent the whole time with one of her friends. I didn't even see my mom or sisters once the walk started.

In the beginning of Covid, my sister reached five years free from breast cancer. I was so happy for her. This was during lockdown when people were doing drive-bys to communicate with friends and relatives. My mom and Tammy wanted me to drive two and a half hours to do a drive-by to congratulate Lisa on being cancer free and then turn around and drive back home.

I asked if I could go into her house to use the bathroom before turning back, and the answer was *no*. Maybe there would be a little table set up on the driveway with some snacks so we could get out of the car and stretch for a little before driving back home?

Again, a big no.

Unconditional Love

So why did I need to drive for over five hours to my sister's house when I couldn't even talk to her or get out of my car to see her? It all sounded ridiculous to me and not something I needed to do to show my sister I was excited for and loved her.

My mom and Tammy called and texted me repeatedly, over and over again for the next three weeks to tell me how important it was for me to be there, how Lisa would be *so* disappointed if I didn't drive by. They pressured and pressured me, and I still did not want to go. And I didn't.

Instead, Bari and I Facetimed Lisa to congratulate her, and we sent her a picture frame with photos of all of us at the breast cancer walk.

That winter, I went on vacation by myself for the first time to Florida. During my time away in Florida, my mom planned to make a settlement on her house. My sisters and I had to Facetime to congratulate her at four p.m. precisely, which meant I had to leave the hotel pool to go back to my room at the specified time. By the way, nobody congratulated me when I sold my house after the divorce.

I made my way up and prepared for Mom's big moment. My sisters had glasses of wine in their hands. I didn't drink all that much, which was why I'd given the champagne away, so I filled my wine glass with water. My sister told me I couldn't have water because it was bad luck. Well, I was in a hotel room and wasn't about to open a $50 bottle from the minibar I wouldn't finish. They insisted it was bad luck to not have a sip of alcohol, and I emphasized that I didn't have any and it would be fine.

When I checked into the hotel, one of the bellhops was extra nice to me and sent a bottle of champagne up to my room. I didn't want it but could hear a few couples on the balcony next to me having a little party. I leaned my head over my balcony and asked if they wanted the champagne. They were *so* excited, and I handed it right over to them. I told my sister this story the day before and she remembered about the bottle of champagne I'd given to my neighbors, and she expected me to knock on their door and ask them for a glass of it back!

Wait, what?

Yes, she was totally serious and repeatedly instructed me to go next door and ask for a little glass. I would *never* do that. Again, I felt uncomfortable for refusing to do what my family ordered me to do.

It's clear I'm not like them. I'm not on the same page as them in any way. I am different and don't fit in. And none of them try to make me feel like I *do* belong, or we are a family and, since my dad is already gone, all we have is each other. None of that.

Chapter Forty-Six:
Lessons Learned

I've learned over the years that I give because it makes me feel good, not to get something back in the future. In fact, I have given without anyone even knowing. Now *that* is true generosity.

Many years later, divorced and driving to work, I heard on the radio somebody had gone into a Target and paid off everyone's layaways for Christmas. I thought that was fabulous! I knew I couldn't possibly pay everyone off, but I could pay for one person. So now I go to my local K-Mart or Marshalls every year at Christmas and pay off somebody's layaway—up to $200. Layaway items are kept in bags in storage, so I can look through them and make sure I'm buying children's clothes and toys. Hanukah isn't anything like Christmas; we don't save all year and splurge. My only stipulation every year is to make sure they write on the receipt that the lucky shopper's secret Santa is a Jew!

It's rewarding. I get so excited thinking about this person going to pick up their items after saving their money, only to find out it's been paid for! Everybody I share this with tells me how amazing it is or how they want to do it too. Except for my mom. When we met for dinner at Marco Polo, an Italian restaurant, and I told her how I paid off someone's layaway for Christmas, instead of saying something endearing, she replied, "You don't have that kind of money." I only wanted my mom to see my generosity and my kindness. I was desperate for her to see the good in me. But her negative reaction let me down again.

Chapter Forty-Seven:
No Reading of the Will?

As a single mom, I know how hard it is to support two kids as well as myself. During Covid, I started to think about how my mom hasn't worked in twenty-five years. Wow, my parents must have had a lot of money for her do that. I also thought about my dad's will. I'd never seen it. In movies, the family sits together while the family attorney reads the will. I don't know what was in my dad's will except that my mom gave me $10,000 when he died. I passed that money right to my husband. My mom also used to ask me to sign checks, and I never questioned her. I just signed with a smile.

I wanted to see my dad's will. I contacted the Registers of Wills, and it took a lot of searching, but they finally found it in the microfiche archives. I learned nothing exciting except the suggestion of trusts being set up (and there are no trusts that I know of for me or my sisters) and the stipulation that each daughter should receive enough money to buy a house or start a business. I guess that was what the $10,000 was for.

Chapter Forty-Eight:
Did I grow up in a different family?

One thing that really affected me occurred when I was at my friend's house for dinner, and they said how sad they were to hear my uncle Marty had died. I was shocked. Nobody, not even my mom, had told me Uncle Marty died. My friends told me he passed away over a year ago. What? I couldn't believe what I was hearing.

As soon as I got home, I called my mom and asked her about Uncle Marty. She told me yes, she knew about it, but she wasn't friends with him or my Aunt Diane anymore. She explained her boyfriend Neil lived behind my uncle Marty and aunt Diane and had had a big argument with them years ago and, because of that, she hadn't spoken to them.

I honestly could not believe was I was hearing. My Aunt Diane and Uncle Marty had been part of my whole life. I have special memories of being at their house in 1974 when the Flyers won the Stanley Cup and swimming in their pool when we were young. Our season tickets to the Flyers games and theirs were three rows apart. I shopped for all my bat mitzvah gifts at Aunt Diane's jewelry counter when I was younger, and she visited me after every one of my surgeries. Their whole family had been there to support us when my dad died. I was devastated I hadn't gone to the funeral or even known about it.

The next morning, I headed straight to my aunt's jewelry store. I walked in and saw her right away, standing at the back of the counter, leaning over and talking on the phone. She recognized me and hung up. By the time I reached the back, I already had tears in my eyes. I told her I hadn't known about Uncle Marty, and I was so sorry I hadn't attended the funeral or Shiva. I cried at how bad I felt to not be there for their kids, who I always loved to see—I even had a big crush on their son while we were growing up. Together, we called her daughter Lisa, and I was able to apologize for not being there for her and her family. This situation heightened my awareness that I was not like my mom or my sisters. None of them even cared. I didn't get it.

Chapter Forty-Nine:
The Letter Again

The past can tick away inside us for decades like a silent time bomb, until it sets off a cellular message that lets us know the body does not forget the past.

—Donna Jackson Nakazawa

During Covid, I found the letter my mom sent me packed up in a box in my basement. She wrote it to me a little over four years after my dad died, and it was so painful to read I had somehow blocked it out in my memory. Sitting on the cold stone floor, reading that letter again as if for the first time, I was brought to tears. But it was that letter that lent me the strength and determination to confront my mom and my sisters once and for all.

Of course, my sisters repeated my mom's words back at me—I had abused her when Daddy died and alienated myself. That was what I had heard for almost twenty years! I did everything I could to try to get along with my family. Attending holiday dinners, adult and children's parties, and other obligatory events. Why had I put myself through that? Because I felt I *had* to; that if I didn't go, my mom and sisters would be even meaner to me.

But it finally reached the point where I just couldn't do it anymore.

Reading Mom's letter again was devastating and brought me back to the raw emotions I'd felt years ago, which I'd suppressed. Eighteen years later, I mustered up enough strength to confront my mom with her letter. She would see how painful it was for me to receive, and I hoped we could move on so we could have a better relationship.

I drove the almost two hours to her place. I had made plans to have lunch with her at her house so I could show her the letter and discuss it with her.

When I got there, the first thing I did was tell Mom I had the letter she wrote to me eighteen years ago, and it really affected the way I saw myself through her eyes. All that time, I'd carried around the disdain my own mother felt toward me. It was also how my sisters viewed me, since they believed everything, she said. In fact, one of my friends calls my sisters Mom's *minions*. My therapist had compared them to the Stepford wives!

I asked her to please read the letter and then we could discuss it because I really needed to talk about it. She sat down in her upholstered armchair and silently scanned the page. I perched on the sofa directly across from her.

When she was done, she looked at me and asked, "Do you want an apology, Stacey?"

I was caught off guard. I'd expected her to feel *some* remorse for the horrible things she'd written. I told her I didn't need an apology, but I did want to her to acknowledge how hurtful it was for me to receive something like that. I told her I couldn't imagine saying any of those things to either of my children. I felt that none of my friends, or anyone who loved me, would ever describe me the way she had.

I'm not negative.

I don't fight with anyone about what they don't do for me.

I *don't* have a mental illness.

I admitted I had a hard time dealing with my dad's death; twenty-five years later, and I have never been the same. But for a parent to put you down and abandon you when you're experiencing the throes of grief—I just didn't understand. If it were me, I'd want to make my children feel better about themselves, not worse.

I explained I needed to get over the letter so we could move forward with a real, honest, loving relationship.

Mom told me she still believed and stood by everything she wrote and would not apologize for anything.

Tears started to fall down my face. She didn't move next to me to put her arm around me in comfort. She just sat there in her armchair, watching me cry without a word.

I told her I could not possibly have a relationship with her anymore if that was the way she felt about me.

She looked at me, shocked but silent. Cold. Empty.

I got up and asked, "Mentally ill?"

Again, she said nothing.

I opened the door and walked out of her house, sobbing. I just couldn't believe she refused to put a letter she wrote eighteen years ago behind us to have a real relationship with her own daughter.

I didn't hear from her until the next night. However, I *did* get a call from my sisters when I got home. They wasted no time in telling me just how much I upset our mom. They were *so* angry at me.

I told them about the letter and all the mean things mom wrote about me all those years ago. Both said they agreed with Mom's assertions. I was devastated.

I must repeat that I am not a negative, unhappy person who has no friends, is mentally ill, and a terrible mother. I am actually a very positive person. As I learned from the plane crash and my dad's passing, life can be so short. It could be gone tomorrow. In a minute. I go out of my way to be nice to people and give back whenever I can. I have a lot of good friends, some I've known since second grade, plus I am a successful attorney.

But what I am most proud of is being a mom.

And my mom's letter makes me out to be a horrible mother. When Dad died, I was pregnant and had a two-year-old. I was a mess. I was severely depressed. But I was not shooting up heroin or screaming and crying to my family about my dad. I was up with them every day, cooked beautiful breakfasts, packed great lunches, and waited at the bus stop with a smile when they came home. Grownups have problems, and kids are resilient. Life isn't a fairytale; it's real. And I know I was a great mom. There are some bad mothers out there, and I am not one of them.

I reached out to my sisters once more to explain again how painful it had been to read that letter. I asked if we could have our own relationship as sisters that didn't involve Mom. They told me it would be impossible. What more was there for me to do?

After my mom refused to apologize or even acknowledge the hurt, she has caused me, I was hysterical and ended up driving straight to Baltimore and staying with my cousin Avi for a few days. She is my person, my friend, the sister I don't have.

Chapter Fifty:
I am Done

Done with trying to figure out who was with her, against her, or walking down the middle because they didn't have the guts to pick a side.
She was done with anything that didn't bring her peace.
She realized that opinions were a dime and dozen, validation was for parking, and loyalty wasn't a word but a lifestyle.
It was this day that her life changed.
And not because of a man or a job but because she realized that life is way too short to leave the key to your happiness in someone else's pocket.

—Carrick Stone

I needed to ask my sisters another question, something that had really upset me all those years: now that we all had kids of our own, could they imagine if one of us suddenly wasn't around and another one had to take their children? Would they be happy if their sister sent their kids to separate boarding schools so far away it took a plane trip to visit?

That still breaks my heart to this day.

Immediately, predictably, my sisters defended my parents' decision and repeated the old line that mom and Dad did thorough research and sent our cousins to the very best schools.

Unconditional Love

"But so far away?" I countered. "Shouldn't they have been close enough to have dinner with family every week or on their birthdays? What if those poor kids missed their parents and were having nightmares from the crash. Shouldn't we have been close enough to be able to comfort them?"

Nope, my sisters did not agree with me. In their minds, Mom and Dad *always* made the right decisions, and that included sending my cousins, who'd just lost their parents in the most horrific way imaginable, away to different boarding schools.

I desperately reached out to my sisters again a little later. I called my sisters to ask, "Why do we hate Uncle Sammy so much?"

One sister replied, "Are you kidding me?" She sounded annoyed and in utter disbelief.

I said, "Really, tell me why we're so mean to him. Give me *one* reason."

They were both shocked I'd even asked the question. They said they refused to discuss it with me and dig up old memories.

I had to gather a lot of strength to ask Mom how she could send my cousins away like that. Bit I did. I called and said, "Mom, I must ask you a question about something that has always upset me. I need to discuss it with you because maybe you can tell me something that will make me understand. Make me feel better."

"Okay. I'm not busy right now. We can talk."

"Why did you send my cousins so far away to boarding school?" I asked. "You had enough money to pay for around-the-clock nannies and cooks to take care of them. So why send them away like that?"

My mom explained that, when my cousins first came to live with us, nobody was getting along. She visited a psychiatrist to discuss the problem, and the psychiatrist told her my cousins would never fit into our "perfect family."

I really can't imagine anyone describing any family as perfect, let alone someone who didn't even know ours!

I pushed some more. "Why did they have to go so far away? So far, you'd have to get on a plane to visit them?"

Again, my mom reiterated her "perfect family" stance and told me she was advised to send my cousins off to boarding school.

I pressed again and shared my thoughts. If they'd been closer, we could've visited if they were having a bad day—which I'd expect they would after losing their parents and being on the plane—could've taken them out to dinner on their birthdays or just on a random Sunday night to be there for them.

My mom replied that that was not how boarding schools worked. You couldn't visit or take them out of school.

I replied, "Don't you think they would have made an exception, given my cousins' tragic situation?"

Unconditional Love

I wasn't getting anywhere with my mom or my sisters. But that was about as much closure as I needed. I got out all the hurt and pain and was finally able to confront them with the deep, honest feelings I've repressed for so many years.

Nobody sees it my way. Nobody wants to even acknowledge that what they did to my cousins may not have been the best idea. Nobody wants to talk to me. Nobody wants to go back.

I can't help it. It haunts me. And I am so tired of looking like the bad one. The one who doesn't get along with any of them. They are toxic. It's their way or no way. You're either in the gang or you're not. I don't want to ever be in that gang again.

Chapter Fifty-One:
My Reading with Danielle Schwartz, Medium

During the difficult times of the Covid pandemic, I felt I needed to be close to Dad again. I wanted to know he was okay and for him to know I was too. I contacted Danielle Schwartz, a well-respected medium. What follows is the transcription of my reading.

***

DS: Let me get a little information without getting information. Are you hoping to connect with loved ones?

SB: Yes.

DS: You have wonderful energy, so I'm excited to connect with you and your family. Hopefully you'll receive some specific messages that will provide you some healing. I connect with the energy of your loved ones. I'm an evidential medium, which means I bring forth a lot of evidence… in the form of personality, possibly names, dates, objects that you may be able to connect with. I do that to give you this "knowing" because, for all you know, I could just be giving you mushy-gushy messages. I work hard on not being led. I want you to leave here today having absolute knowing…

SB: I'll follow your lead.

DS: Try to see the faces of loved ones you wish to connect with. Take another deep breath. I have two individuals here. I'm going to start with the female because she has a really big energy, very, very protective of you. Feels like Grandmom or Mom. Do you have a grandmom or mom in spirit?

SB: I have Grandmom.

DS: It's on Dad's side. That's why she said, "I'm with him." She just pulled him through, but he's very respectful of his mom, of his parents. I want to bring through Dad—is that who you would welcome messages from?

SB: Yes.

DS: I absolutely love his energy. He makes me want to smile. I feel like he had a quirky personality; he was an acquired taste, he's telling me. I feel the two of you had a really, really great relationship, because he's making me feel energetically very close to you. In fact, if it were up to him, I'd be going through the computer and giving you a big hug. He wants you to know he's around, he's around all the kids. He's not gone anywhere, he's around everyone—he's wanting me to tell you that. And he's telling me that he did suffer quite a bit. It's like we were prepared but we weren't prepared; he's saying that it happened very fast. He had been dealing with things a lot. He's telling me his legs are all better—that's something he wants you to know. He's telling me that something happened with his circulation... Can you understand all that?

SB: Not necessarily his legs.

DS: There's something with organs shutting down and fluid...

SB: That was his heart.

DS: He was supposed to have a procedure, there was something with a procedure, and then something happened, and it got worse—but he needs everyone to know we did everything we could. That's important. I feel like he wants to give you guys reassurance that there was nothing else that could have been done.

SB: When you say, "you guys," who are you referring to other than me?

DS: The family. Together, you had some decisions to make, some tough choices. And I feel like some of you are still holding on, according to what he's saying. Like, "Did we do everything we can?" I have another pretty prominent female. Were your parents still married? Mom was very much involved. He needs you to know he still watches out for her. He's also showing me the clothes... You actually have a shirt that's hanging up in the closet?

SB: Yes.

DS: Just know that when you hold onto that, he's there. He wants you to know that. He's also telling me that you feel him. But you question that: "Are you really there?" And he's saying, "It's really me," and he's also telling me that you talk to him all the time. He's around your kids, he's loves them so much. He's so proud of them, And he's so proud of you. He is showing me the ring as being something that's significant. Does someone still have the ring?

SB: I wear two of them.

DS: Did you have them fixed or readjusted?

SB: Yes.

DS: Just know that's something he's aware of, and when you hold onto them, he says you need to know "I'm with you." And he's also saying, "Thank you for holding my hand, thank you for everything that you did." I feel you were very near his face. I want you to know he's coming through very handsome and very charming. There's this photograph of him when he was younger, and that's how he wants to be remembered. But he says, "I wasn't always easy" —that's something he would like to apologize for: for not being more vocal with how he feels. I see the two of you talking, these conversations you guys would have, and I do feel like he was very much your biggest supporter, so please know that he's still your biggest cheerleader. He said, "I need her to know I'm always around her." He's showing me being outside, something with the gatherings outside—as being something that would be significant. I don't know if that's his house that had the big outside space or yours. The family gatherings were something that he would really love. He just loved that. He loved being with the family—his family is everything. I have a very hard worker here. His work was something that was very important to him. And I do feel that he looked out for everyone. He's a very humble individual, would not brag about himself. It made him feel good to take care of everyone, that's what made him feel good. He's still doing that from where he is. He's got a great smile, but I guess something happened with his teeth on one side or something like that. He has his big smile back. He's talking a lot, and I feel he would have talked so much when he was here. He's more of a listener, and he would add some things. But right now, he's so excited to actually be able to talk to you that his energy is back. I don't know if he was on oxygen, but he's telling me everything was an effort, and it's not anymore. And he wants you to know where he is. He's surrounded… his parents are in spirit, so know that they are with him. I also feel that he has a brother in spirit with him… so know that they are together. And that is something that has brought his heart a lot of healing. He's also showing me his wallet. There's something with his ID, and then he's showing me—Mom has it. Does Mom have it?

SB: I don't know.

DS: He's also showing me something with the same picture…

SB: There's a picture that was in his wallet of me and him. I have the picture.

DS: And that's something you actually carry?

SB: Yes. It's in my wallet, now.

DS: He needs you to know when you look at that, he's with you. He's also showing me the phone, and I feel like we have messages, something with a message… I hear your dad's voice. When you listen to his voice, he needs you to

Unconditional Love

know he is still there. He's also saying you have photographs of him nearby... He said that he's still in the chair. There's this one space that he's still in, like *his* chair, and that's something that would be important for him to let you guys know. Because, when you feel that energetically, he wants you to know he's there. And there's something about the blanket, some significance with this blanket, or sweater, or sweatshirt because I feel like it's giving me warmth. There's a blanket on the back of the chair? Or on the couch. In the room where the TV is. Is Mom still in the same house?

SB: No. He had a special chair, but he didn't have a special blanket.

DS: Does someone still have the chair?

SB: I don't think so.

DS: Was it a recliner?

SB: Yes.

DS: I just feel like it was special to him. Like he just really loved that chair. Almost like Archie Bunker's chair.

SB: Yes—he was like Archie Bunker!

DS: That's why he's showing me Archie Bunker. I do feel like he could be a little on the gruff side, but inside he was this big teddy bear. Especially toward his older days. I feel like the grandkids gave him this opportunity to be really sweet. And that is something he is happy to have had, that experience.

SB: He *didn't* really get to see the grandkids.

DS: He's showing me the picture with the baby.

SB: Just one.

DS: Was that your son?

SB: Yes.

DS: Is there a photograph of him where he's holding the baby?

SB: Somewhere around here.

DS: Is he named after your dad? Like a middle name?

SB: My daughter is named after him.

DS: Just know that he wants you to know he's seen her. He hasn't missed anything. When he says he's had this opportunity to be by their side, that's because he has been. He hasn't missed a birthday; he hasn't missed an anniversary—he needs you to know he's seen it all. That is so important for him. I also feel that he really protects your heart. And he's telling me that you haven't had it easy, and you do a lot for the family to try to keep everybody together, and he says, "I just need you to know that I know what you do, and I know it hasn't been easy." Does your mother live in close proximity to you?

SB: No. Not really. Like an hour.

DS: Is she very independent? Is she very busy, stubborn, that kind of thing?

SB: Yes.

Unconditional Love

DS: Dealing with your mom, he wants you to understand what you go through. Again, he's so incredibly proud of who you are. He's also bringing me to… I have this box… There's some photos in there, some cards. Some things with his writing, there's different things. Just know that box… "Even when you just see that box, you think of me," he's telling me. Were you in your twenties when he passed? Or thirties?

SB: I was thirty.

DS: It's important for your dad that you know he's always been by your side. He also keeps bringing up this watch that's significant.

SB: Yes.

DS: Who has the watch?

SB: My sister.

DS: Is that something that's been a source of contention? He just says he understands.

SB: Am I supposed to tell you about the watch?

DS: That's up to you. It's the third time he's brought up the watch. There's some kind of tension around this watch. Maybe she's thinking of giving it to someone else? Just tension.

SB: Yes. It's just annoying. I asked for the watch when he passed away, twenty-three years ago, and my mom kept it in a box. And then my sister just recently asked for it, and she just gave it to her. But I got the rings.

DS: He wants you to know he understands. Is there someone in Florida? Because he's showing me water and the beach.

SB: My son.

DS: Know that he is around him. Even though he was a baby when he passed—he keeps calling him the baby—he has watched out for you kids. He is their guardian angel. This is coming from your dad—you have amazing kids. Is he in his twenties?

SB: Yes.

DS: Is your daughter about to turn twenty-three?

SB: She is twenty-three.

DS: I just feel like good things are coming for her. She's a really hard worker. Your dad wants you to celebrate that and know that he sees it. I know it's been a while since he passed, but he says, "You still talk to me." There's this one picture where you say, "Hey, Dad, how are you? What are you doing?" He keeps going back to your heart, just giving healing to the heart. Emotional healing to the heart. There's a lot of things you've had to do on your own. He's so incredibly proud of you. Did your father own his own business?

SB: Yes.

DS: Is that business still present?

SB: No.

DS: Just know that he's okay with that. Are you in a committed relationship? Are you married?

SB: Divorced.

DS: That's where I keep going back with the heart. I don't feel that you are honored, according to your dad. He's happy that you're standing up for you. You ask him, "All right, Dad, what now? What do you think?" He is looking out for you, so if you do decide you want to trust the male species again, know that is something he will help you through. Imagine introducing your husband to your father... Are you dating?

SB: I try!

DS: Do you own a shore house?

SB: We did.

DS: I keep seeing you by the water. I see you happy by the water. I feel that was something that was really important for your dad; that was his space as well. Is Mom remarried?

SB: No.

DS: Is she in a relationship?

SB: Not right now. She was. A couple times.

DS: It just feels like this past relationship, or the one before it, is not finished. The only reason Dad brings that up is because he feels that relationship is not for her highest good. There is something with the trust, or the money, the finances, that we need to watch out for with Mom. He doesn't want her to get taken advantage of. I get this energy like she's the puppet.

SB: You mean someone is puppeteering her?

DS: Yes.

SB: No.

DS: She's the puppeteer?

SB: Yes.

DS: As far as her not releasing the money... I just feel like I'm holding onto it.

SB: Could it be the boyfriend's money?

DS: It could be. Let me tell you exactly what I'm hearing: it's almost as if you've needed support in the past, and you've been made to feel guilty or it's not been easy to ask for support, and you haven't gotten that support. I just don't feel that your mom has been easy to deal with or there's been some challenges with you needing some support. There's this wish that, if Dad were still here, things would be different. He was in your corner. Where your mom and your sister were in cahoots, and then it was like you had Dad. Then he passed, and it was: "Who do I have? Now I'm on my own." He said, "I need you to know something. You're gonna be okay. I've got your back." He promises you're gonna be okay. He promises that you're gonna be happy. I do have to go back to his passing… I feel like I have to clear some things up, according to what he's saying to me. He's saying you were there. But there are these questions: "Are we sure we should do that? Are we sure we shouldn't do that?" I feel like you're on your own trying to advocate for your dad, where your mom and your sister were over here… and you were dealing with that on your own. You still hold a lot of guilt, he's saying. Did you fight enough? He needs you to know you did everything you could. He's telling me he would have never been the same, had he survived.

SB: All the things you are saying are true.

DS: It feels like you and your dad are soulmates. Not only did you lose your dad, you lost the one person who really got you and was in your corner. He needs you to know: "You didn't lose me." There is this phrase, saying, like a term of endearment I want to share with you from him. He's showing me this sunflower and keeps saying, "She's my sunshine." You were his light. He's trying to explain the dynamics of the family. He's like a mediator. He understood and loved everyone in your family. You and your dad just got each other. I feel maybe your mom and your sister had some jealousy about the relationship you had or didn't understand it. Your sense of humor is the same; your mom and sister are looking at him like, "What's funny?" and you're rolling on the ground. You got it. That caused a divide between the three of you. And he's very sad about that. He wants you all to be together. He knows that you have tried and tried, and you've been misunderstood. It got borderline toxic for a while, which is why you had to pull back. He feels like you were unnecessarily attacked. Your dad is trying to push you all together. He's saying, "You're family; you don't have to like each other, but you do have to love each other." He knows you've tried and is not blaming you; he's just trying to bring healing because he knows how much you hurt. I want to talk about the signs because he's like, "You wonder where I am, what I'm doing, when I'm with you." Numbers seem to be something that's really significant… He says he sends you repeated numbers. That means 111, 222, 333—all one number. Is there a connection with April or the number four?

SB: No.

DS: When you see that repeated number, just know it's a sign coming through from him. He said he sends you songs all the time. So when you hear a song that reminds you of him, that's his way to let you know he's with you. He has a corny sense of humor. He kept showing me this bowling ball: "I'm bowling with the angels."

SB: I used to tell my kids, when it was a really bad thunderstorm, that Pops was bowling with the angels!

DS: He showed me that bowling ball three times; so persistent. He wants you to know he really hasn't missed anything, and when you were talking with your kids, he heard everything. I really need to leave you with a message of hope, according to what he's saying… From your dad, good things are coming; you may have some bumps. Just ride through it and know that in a year, quite possibly sooner, good things are coming. I do feel that you are going to be able to move. I do see you near water; I see you laughing by the water with a relationship that feels comfortable. Again, imagine introducing them to your dad…

Chapter Fifty-Two:
Fly Away

> *I'm not going to continue knocking on that old door that doesn't open for me. I am going to create my own door and walk through that.*
>
> —Ava DuVernay

The past twenty-five years of trying to get along with my family had been tremendously difficult for me. I've decided I can't do it anymore. I can't go to another family dinner where we eat latkes with fat-free sour cream. You're already eating fried potatoes, for goodness sakes! And you only make them once a year! And nobody even gets *regular* sour cream as an option for me.

I don't want to go to any more of their parties and feel uncomfortable. I don't want to be around anyone who makes me feel the way they do. I only want to spend time with people who love me and make me feel good about myself.

My daughter had moved in with her boyfriend and was no longer living with me. It was the perfect time to move.

So, I sold everything in Philadelphia, packed it up, and moved to Miami! To get away from them. To live free from their judgement. To no longer "have to do" what my mom says.

I not only moved to get away from my family, but also to get away from being Waxman's ex-wife and stop constantly running into Marla (who he cheated on me with), Marla's friends (who were also some of my friends), Jody (his new wife), and her friends. I didn't want to have to be strong all the time and act like a lady anymore. I was tired of Marla asking me how my kids were while feeling as if everyone in the restaurant was looking at me.

One time, when I was at the salon, the girl washing my hair associated me with Jon's sister, my ex-sister-in-law, Melissa, who used to work at the salon. (In fact, she started working at the salon the week before I found out Jon was cheating on me, and I sent her a beautiful arrangement of yellow roses so her makeup counter would look extra pretty on her first week of work.) As she washed my hair, she asked how Melissa was. As Melissa had played a huge part in Jon's cheating, I once again had to act like a lady and nicely say I had not spoken with her.

The girl replied, "I'm sorry, are you friends with the wife?"

I looked up at her, with my head in the sink, and said, "I *am* the wife."

Those are the kinds of things I just could not get away from.

To validate my feelings even further, after I decided to move to Miami and put my house up for sale in Philly, I tried to sell what I couldn't bring with me. A couple came to my house to view my outdoor furniture. As I opened the door and greeted them, the first thing the woman said to her husband was, "Doesn't she look like Waxman's ex?"

At that point, I had to say, "I *am* Waxman's ex," and that made me realize I was doing the right thing by moving; I *had* to get out of there. I left with no job and no friends. But I'd also moved to be near my son Josh in Brickel.

Now I live in Miami, and Jacob and Martine's daughter Kareen also lives here. I reach out to her, and we make plans to meet up. She loves my parents as much as I love hers. They had three daughters, as did the Bergers, and Kareen and I were both the oldest. We are always so happy to see each other and share so many lovely memories.

Now in Miami, I was invited to her son's bar mitzvah and, while there, I got to see Martine and Jacob. I was *so* excited and couldn't wait! The next day, they invited me for lunch at their home on Fisher Island. Just going to Fisher Island was an experience all in itself: you can only access the island by ferry. You must actually drive your car onto the ferry. And you can't even get on the ferry without someone putting your name on the list!

Over lunch, Jacob and Martine told me Mom told them she could no longer be friends with them. They said they were shocked and *very* upset. They just did not understand why.

A lightbulb went off in my head: something that maybe explained all of this hurt I carried. How hard could it possibly be for my mom to have a friendship with someone in Paris, in another country? It wasn't like she had to blow them off to meet for coffee every week! Telling old friends, she couldn't talk to them anymore was understandably upsetting and bewildering!

Unconditional Love

But maybe it explains why Mom can't be nice to me either. I believe it's too painful for her to talk to friends of almost fifty years because they remind her of my dad. Well, guess who else must remind her of my dad?

Me!

Personally, I want to keep *everything* that reminds me of my childhood and Dad, while my mom and sisters don't care about getting rid of all of it. That has been the foundation of all my problems with Mom.

I *am* my dad.

I want to embrace and remember everything, whereas my mom wants to forget. So much so, she can't bear to talk to friends of over fifty years who live across the world in another country.

That was the first time I maybe understood why my mom is so cold to me. Maybe I just remind her too much of my dad, and she wants to forget. At least I have something, a little closure, to make me feel a bit better and to comprehend why she treats me the way she does.

It has become very clear to me that, when my dad died, I turned into Cinderella. Before, it was the king—my dad—and me, his lieutenant. Now the king is dead, and I have been put in the metaphorical basement.

I *am* the family's Cinderella.

Well, it's out of the basement and into an ocean-view apartment in Miami. I'm living my best life with the cards I've been dealt. I'm still looking for Prince Charming, but even though I am alone, I am not lonely. I have gone on so many dates, and it's exhausting. I don't have a list of must-haves like a lot of girls—all I want is a relationship to be easy and comfortable. Otherwise, I choose to be by myself.

In fact, I bet a lot of couples out there *wish* they were alone. I am not going to live my life bickering with someone or trying to be something I am not.

And now, my daughter has moved to Miami and lives with me, which means I have both my children here. From day one, they have been the most important thing in my life.

What more can I ask?

Epilogue

It is not only a matter, I believe, of religious observance and practice. To me, being Jewish means and has always meant being proud to be part of a people that has maintained its distinct identity for more than 2,000 years, with all the pain and torment that has been inflicted upon it.

—Golda Meir

Before the terrible events of October 7, 2024, I was aware of antisemitism and that some people didn't like us. I grew up seeing my elementary school painted with swastikas, being thrown into the lockers in high school, and there was that time I'd been left on the golf course on my honeymoon! All because I was Jewish.

My kids have also experienced antisemitism growing up. My son was called a "Jew boy" on the basketball court in elementary school, and my daughter was told by her friend she wouldn't be allowed to play with her if her mom knew she was Jewish.

It is very interesting to me that, as Jewish people, we do not reply in anger or public protests but just accept the hate. My parents didn't go to school to complain I was being physically and mentally attacked because of my religion. And I returned to school every day, petrified of one girl who threw me into the lockers if she saw me in the hallways. I also did not call school when my son was called a Jew boy on school property. I just told him his friend didn't know what he was saying. I told him to always be proud of who he was, and we moved on.

Unconditional Love

I can't imagine if someone had called a black child something so racist. There would be protests and news broadcasts of the deplorable actions. However, Jews just don't do that. We endure the hate, and I am not sure why. We sweep such occurrences under the rug, and nobody really talks about it.

When I make friends outside of my Jewish circle and relate my experiences with antisemitism, they simply cannot believe it. Nobody is aware we are disliked just because we are Jewish. But thanks to our upbringings, we also sweep our feelings under that rug and are only left with the pride of being Jewish.

I explain to my gentile friends that when I go somewhere, I am well aware I am not "white," even though the difference may not be as apparent as having black skin. Like an Italian, Spanish, Greek, or even Arab person, I am most definitely not "white." I can go into any restaurant and see there are no Jews with one glance.

In 2015, I drove to Raleigh, North Carolina with Avi to see the Rolling Stones in concert. As we got farther south and finally arrived at our destination, we very clearly stood out. We were asked if we were from New York, we looked so different!

I have experienced antisemitism my whole life, but I continued to ignore the hate and to be proud of my Jewish identity. After October 7, this hatred for the Jewish people has become frightening. While I grew up looking the other way from the hate I received, events today are very different. Prejudice is thrown in my face, like a strong, rushing wave. I feel tossed under the water by a steady tide trying to drag me down and keep me under. I'm in shock and struggling to surface for air.

Do my gentile friends see my struggle?

Will anyone help me out of the ocean of hatred?

Nobody comes.

None of my friends acknowledge the pain and fear I experience as this unmasked hate is displayed on every news channel. There are protests in cities across the world demanding for Israel to be destroyed "from the river to the sea," and crowds chanting, "Death to the Jews!" Those protesters not only want to kill all the Jews, but they support Hamas. It is Hamas who are the terrorists who've been holding the innocent Palestinians hostage since October 7. Hamas have tortured, raped, and murdered innocent people. They continue to abuse and torture the hostages, some of them American, they have held in captivity for over six months.

Colleges and universities across America, prestigious schools with supposedly intelligent students, are now "hubs" for this Jewish hatred. Some schools are private institutions, on private land, so the local police cannot enter the property without the school's specific request and approval. All administration needs to do is ask the local police department for help, and the protesters would be dispersed. Why aren't they doing that?

Jewish students who worked and studied so hard to get into these Ivy League schools and who are paying so much money to attend are petrified to walk around campus. I heard the story of one Jewish girl whose roommate, who was once her good friend, has now turned into one of the protesters. The Jewish student is afraid to stay in her own dorm room and has left campus to live with her grandmother.

How is this even happening in 2024?

I taught seventh grade Jewish Studies in the Hebrew High School, and part of my curriculum was the Holocaust. My students were twelve- and thirteen-year-olds, and I would ask them, "What would you do if you went into the cafeteria for lunch, and they told you all Jewish kids now must sit at another table, separated from everyone else?" And there really isn't an answer.

Many Jewish people have taken off any jewelry depicting Stars of David, chaos, or mezuzahs. Jews have always been advised to take such symbols off when traveling to certain countries; we are used to it and know of the hatred out there.

But not in America.

Don't forget that the Jews in Germany were doctors and lawyers who believed nothing bad could ever happen to them because they were smart, educated, and hard-working.

Then look at what happened…

The Holocaust.

***

I decided to call my book *Unconditional Love*, as it applies to my mom and my sisters' love for me as being very *conditional*. I truly believe the same can be said for the gentile world and its relationship with the Jewish people. We are just like everyone else, but sometimes we make friends, we meet people… only to discover, when they find out we are Jewish, the love we've forged is no longer unconditional.

***

I also want this book to serve as an inspiration for those dealing with a dysfunctional family, grief, loss and/or divorce. Despite whatever life throws at us, we still only get one life on this earth. This is not a dress rehearsal. And EVERY DAY IS A BLESSING!!! Life is short and can be gone tomorrow. As I have firsthand experience. If you do not have any **choice or control** over the situation, you must let it go.

If your husband cheats and doesn't want to be with you anymore, why would you want to be with him? He doesn't want you. There is a whole world out there and someone is going to tell you how pretty, smart and funny you are. That is what everyone deserves to hear.

If your family judges you, makes you feel uncomfortable and is toxic, walk away. You don't have time for that. I spent over 25 years of my life telling my mom and sisters how uncomfortable I was around them and how I felt like an outcast in my own family after dad died. But they continued to judge, attack and hurt me.

I wish I had walked away sooner. I wish I had gone to one less party. I wish I never listened to my mom and gave my dad's necklace to my sister. I wish I had been nicer to my grandparents and my Uncle Sammy and Aunt Tris. I wish I had called Dr. Nakhjavan. I wish so many things had been different.

Surround yourself with people that make you feel good about yourself and truly love you. Learn to love yourself and do things that make you happy. Your happiness should not be dependent on someone else. It might look bad to be alone, but you do not have to be lonely! I would never want to go back to my marriage or my family just to have their company. I live in peace and happiness.

Made in the USA
Columbia, SC
18 February 2025

39812dbd-3830-454f-8d75-afc8d7c98b39R03